Skylight

David Hare was born in Sussex in 1947. His first play
Slag, was produced in 1970. A year later, he first worked
at the National Theatre, beginning one of the longest
relationships of any playwright with a contemporary
theatre. Since *Plenty* in 1978, the National has presented
eleven of his plays. He has also written four original films
for television. The first of his six feature films, *Wetherby*,
which he also directed, won the Golden Bear at Berlin in
1985.

by the same author

plays
SLAG
THE GREAT EXHIBITION
KNUCKLE
BRASSNECK (with Howard Brenton)
FANSHEN
TEETH 'N' SMILES
PLENTY
A MAP OF THE WORLD
PRAVDA (with Howard Brenton)
THE BAY AT NICE and WRECKED EGGS
THE SECRET RAPTURE
RACING DEMON
MURMURING JUDGES
THE ABSENCE OF WAR
AMY'S VIEW

screenplays for television
LICKING HITLER
DREAMS OF LEAVING
SAIGON: YEAR OF THE CAT
HEADING HOME

screenplays
PLENTY
WETHERBY
PARIS BY NIGHT
STRAPLESS
THE SECRET RAPTURE

opera libretto
THE KNIFE

prose
WRITING LEFT-HANDED
ASKING AROUND: BACKGROUND TO THE DAVID HARE TRILOGY

DAVID HARE

Skylight

faber and faber
LONDON · BOSTON

by
... London WC1N 3AU

...vice, Leicester
...itain by
...am, Kent

© David Hare, 1995

David Hare is hereby identified as author of this work in accordance with the
Copyright, Designs and Patents Act 1988.

All rights whatsoever in this play are strictly reserved and applications to
perform it should be made in writing, before rehearsals begin, to Casarotto
Ramsay Company, National House, 60–66 Wardour Street,
London W1Z 3HP.

A CIP record for this book
is available from the British Library

ISBN 0–571–17612–7

6 8 10 9 7 5

For Nicole
à la folie

We had fed the heart on fantasies,
The heart's grown brutal from the fare.

Characters

Kyra Hollis
Edward Sergeant
Tom Sergeant

Skylight was first performed at the Cottesloe, National Theatre, London, on 4 May 1995. The cast was as follows:

Kyra Hollis Lia Williams
Edward Sergeant Daniel Betts
Tom Sergeant Michael Gambon

Director Richard Eyre
Designer John Gunter
Lighting Mark Jonathan

Act One

SCENE ONE

A first-floor flat in north-west London. There is a corniced plaster ceiling, and underneath the evidence of a room well lived in: patterned carpets which have worn to a thread and a long wall of books. The kitchen area at the back of the room looks cluttered and much used. There is a main entrance on to the landing outside. Off to the other side, a bedroom and bathroom.

At once through the main door comes **Kyra Hollis**. *She is just past thirty. She is returning to her flat, blue with cold. She is quite small, with short hair and a practical manner. She has a heavy overcoat wrapped round her, and is wearing thick woollen gloves. She is carrying three large plastic bags. She puts two down at once on her work table and takes the third into the kitchen area. She takes out a packet of spaghetti and some tins of tomatoes. Then she turns, not taking her coat off as she comes through the main room again. She goes on through into the bedroom. The sound offstage of the bath being turned on. In the kitchen, an Ascot flares.*

At the main door, which is still open, a tall young man appears. He is eighteen. He has blue jeans, leather gloves and a denim jacket. He has turned the collar up against the cold. He has a Walkman round his neck. He is also carrying three plastic bags. His name is **Edward Sergeant**. *He comes in a pace or two, then stands, uncertain, hearing the sound of the bath.*

After a moment, Kyra *reappears on her way back to her shopping bag. She looks across the room, taken aback.*

Edward The door was open . . .

Kyra My goodness.

They stand a moment, both lost for what to say next. Then she gestures back offstage.

Just hold on a minute, I'd started running a bath.

She goes out. He stands, still not coming further into the room. Then she reappears.

Edward It's my fault.

Kyra No.

Edward I shouldn't have called in like this. I've grown. Yeah, I know. Everyone says that.

Kyra How tall are you?

But as he blushes, before he can answer, she moves towards him.

Well, will you give me a kiss?

She kisses his cheek. Then he raises his plastic bags.

Edward I brought these.

Kyra What's this?

Edward Some beer. It's a present.

Kyra Thank you.

Edward And some rap records. I don't know how much you know about this stuff.

Kyra Nothing.

Edward I just spent £30 in that shop round the corner. That's why I'm here. It's next to the Nepalese restaurant. There's this great specialist rap shop. All my friends go there. Then I realized you must live round here.

Kyra That's right. I do.

Edward waits, not knowing what to say.

Edward I had the spare time. I'm in my gap year. If you know what I mean.

Kyra Yes, of course.

Edward Out of school, not yet at university. I'm doing what everyone does.

Kyra You have a job?

Edward Yeah. I'm selling frankfurters outside football grounds. If you come close you can smell them.

Kyra It's all right, thanks, I'll stay over here.

She smiles, but she still has not asked him to sit down.

Edward It's freezing.

Kyra I know. Close the door. You gave me a shock standing there.

Edward (*as he closes the door*) I'm feeling embarrassed.

Kyra Why?

Edward I've never done this.

Kyra Hold on, I've got a small fire in here.

Edward looks round nervously, as she gets a small electric fire out and plugs it in.

Edward It's a very nice place.

Kyra My God! You are growing up. When did you start saying dumb things like that? 'It's a very nice place!' When I knew you, Edward, you always spoke your mind. You came to the point.

Edward Ah. OK. The point is my father.

Kyra has a glimmer of humour, as if she is about to reply.

3

But instead she stands up and looks at the miserable one-bar fire.

Kyra I've plugged it in. I think you'll find it makes very little difference. The last few weeks it's been so damp I find you barely see it. Here, we even have indoor fog. You sit on that side of the room and peer, thinking, I'm sure it's on, I'm sure the fire *is* on. But you can't actually see. Do you want tea?

Edward No, thank you.

Kyra So why not tell me what you came here to say?

She rubs her mittens together, still on the opposite side of the room. It seems more like Russia than England.

Edward I'm not sure what you know. Did you know my mother had died?

Kyra I knew she had cancer. How long ago?

Edward It's about a year now.

Kyra A year?

Edward Dad hasn't told you?

Kyra I haven't seen him.

Edward That's why I came here today. I wasn't passing by . . .

Kyra No.

Edward I don't suppose anyone does. Pass by this area, I mean. Unless, I suppose, they're desperate to get from Willesden to South Finchley. Which I can't imagine most people are.

Kyra sits, not reacting to this familiar satire about her address.

Did you . . . I mean, you lost your parents . . .

4

Kyra I did. My father recently. My mother died young. I barely knew her.

Edward Once they're dead, I find they keep changing. You think you've got hold of them. And it's like you say, 'Oh I see. So that's what she was like.' But then they change again in your memory. It drives you crazy. Now I'd like to find out just who she was.

Kyra Alice?

Edward Yes. It's also . . . you see . . . I don't know . . . it's had an effect on my father.

Kyra Why, surely.

Edward I mean if you see him . . . I'd love it. I mean, if you did.

Kyra Why?

Edward Because he's changed.

Kyra And?

She is giving nothing away. He becomes more nervous again.

Edward Now I'm really embarrassed. I'm guessing. I think you can help him.

Kyra Help Tom? Tom needs help?

Edward Well, at least that's what I think.

Kyra is still so silent he is unnerved.

The tea actually . . . I would like the tea now. I'd like some tea to help get me through.

He laughs at this sudden admission of his own nervousness and Kyra too seems to relax as she gets up to put the kettle on.

How am I doing? Am I doing all right?

Kyra You're doing fine.

Edward You don't think I'm being obnoxious? I mean, it's none of my business. If you want you can send me away.

Kyra You can say what you like. It's not going to bother me.

Edward I don't really know the whole history. I mean, between Dad and you.

Kyra Ah. So is that why you're here?

Edward No, I mean, yes, well, partly. But also Dad's got very peculiar. I am here for his sake as well. (*He has started to pace round the room.*) It can get pretty strange, I promise you. Silence at dinner, that kind of thing. We moved to Wimbledon.

Kyra My God!

Edward I know. Well, that doesn't help. The sense of all that sort of *nature*, trees and flowers, sort of flapping around. He did it for Mum, to give her some peace at the end. But now it just seems pointless and spooky. Me, I get on a bus and head for the street.

Kyra brings mugs and teabags.

I keep saying, Dad, you're not dead, you're fifty. It's too early for lupins. Jesus! What I liked about Dad, he was sort of ageless. I think that's why he was such a success. All ages, all types. He knew how to reach them. But now he's in this kind of hideous green fortress.

Kyra Does he talk to you? About what he feels?

Edward You know Dad. He's not what you might call 'emotionally available'. But also . . . let's face it . . . well, I can be quite a shit. (*He faces Kyra directly.*) Have you read Freud?

6

Kyra Some.

Edward I read some recently. I told Dad everything had to come out. That you pay a price. Is that true?

Kyra I don't know.

Edward For everything you repress there's a price to be paid.

Kyra You told him that?

Edward Yes.

Kyra And how did he take it?

But Edward is too preoccupied even to notice her question.

Edward It was the night before last. It was Sunday. We had the mother of all arguments. We had the most terrible row. I suppose I left home.

Kyra You did? Where did you go? Do you have a girlfriend?

Edward Sort of. There's a girl who's willing to take me in. She does the frankfurters with me. (*Suddenly he starts defending himself from some unspoken attack.*) So. I don't know. I'm only eighteen. I don't like the word 'girlfriend'. All that stuff's finished. Relationships. Permanence. It's out of date, I think. I stayed there last night. I'll stay there tonight.

Kyra Yes, but have you rung your father?

Edward looks at her resentfully, turning the question aside with a joke.

Edward She's the only girl who'll sleep with me. Because at least we both smell the same.

Kyra goes back to get the boiling kettle.

7

Dad is a fuckpig. I mean it. I don't think you see it. I talked
to some people at work. He commands respect, yes of
course. People who have all that confidence do. But you
scratch the surface, you talk to his employees, you find
respect can be much more like fear . . .

*Kyra returns with the kettle and starts pouring for both of
them.*

There's one woman, you know, I happened to talk to her, it
was by chance, she's pretty high up, she's worked close to
Dad for some time. She knows him well. And she said he is
definitely sexist.

Kyra No!

Edward She said without question.

Kyra Thank God she spotted it. Milk?

Edward Oh, so, OK, what are you saying? You think it's
me, it's just me being stupid . . .

Kyra No . . .

Edward Father–son. That sort of thing. There's a whole list
of things I could tell you. Dad can be a real bastard you
know. (*He holds up a finger and thumb.*) The charm's that
deep.

Kyra Are you keeping an inventory?

Edward All right, but you don't have to live with it, you
don't have to deal with anyone at all . . . (*He waves airily
round the flat.*) I do. There's always this doom. This
heaviness. He comes home every night. Wham! He lands on
the sofa. You feel the springs go. One night he actually
destroyed a whole sofa. He cracked a sofa he landed so
hard! Then –

Kyra Sugar?

8

Edward Guess his response? Guess his response to it! Next day he just bought a new sofa! A new sofa!

Kyra Well, that seems fair enough.

Edward No, you're wrong. It's an attitude, Kyra. It's all *Yellow Pages*. Whatever. Leaves on the roof? *Yellow Pages!* The lavatory's blocked? *Yellow Pages!* That's how he lives. He even orders in meals. It's absurd! He flicks through. Pizza! Chinese! It's *Citizen Kane!* Only with *Yellow Pages*. I said to him, Dad, for God's sake get real. Not everything in life is in *Yellow Pages*.

Kyra is just drinking her tea.

Kyra Isn't it grief?

Edward Yes, of course.

Kyra He's grieving.

Edward He's sitting there alone in this bloody great house. Like some stupid animal. Licking his pain. (*He turns towards her, more tentative as he talks of his mother.*) Mum . . . of course, I mean, everyone said to me . . . Alice wasn't as clever as him. People assumed she was some sort of dumb ex-model. But she kept Dad moving. Now he just sits there. (*He is vehement, trying to drive his pain away.*) I say for Christ's sake, it's been almost a year. And three years' illness. We knew it was coming. It's been a long time. Let it out, for fuck's sake. Because, I tell you, otherwise . . . it's driving us both bloody mad.

Kyra Are you alone now? What's happened to your sister?

Edward We're like a married couple. Hilary's gone to university.

Kyra Already? So she's on her way.

Edward That's what I'm saying. We're both off. We're

finished. Almost. Next year, I mean. I've got my CV.

Kyra Ugh.

She grimaces at the mention of the word.

Edward I think I'm going to read CV when I get there. As my special subject. Why not? Nobody does anything because we might actually enjoy it. We do it so we can all write it down. Then just wave this absurd bit of paper . . .

Kyra laughs as he waves an imaginary piece of paper.

All right, I know, it's stupid, but you just tell me, what choice do I have?

Kyra You? You have none.

Edward What do your kids do?

Kyra Mine? Oh well, they're different.

Edward You're teaching in East Ham?

Kyra Uh-huh.

Edward How is that?

Kyra East Ham? Well, it has its drawbacks. I wouldn't say the kids are all great. But at least they're not on the ladder. So perhaps that means . . . they do things for their own sake.

Edward Yeah.

Kyra You don't need a CV to get a UB40.

At once Edward leans forward, intrigued.

Edward No, well exactly, I mean *exactly*. As you say, it's different.

Kyra It is.

Edward The fact is . . . when I think about that kind of life

. . . just ordinary kids . . . I know it sounds stupid, but I feel sort of envious.

Kyra Do you?

Edward I suppose you think I'm just spoilt.

Kyra No.

Edward I'm not saying . . . God knows . . . that my life is too easy, nobody could live alone with my bastard of a father and say that my life is easy at all . . . But I do look at the street, and think shit! Shit! And here am I heading in exactly the opposite direction.

Kyra just watches as he gestures rather randomly round the flat.

I mean, I think in a way you're so lucky, living like this . . .

Kyra Well, thank you.

Edward I'm not being rude. I mean it. In this kind of place. (*He pauses a second.*) Dad said . . .

Kyra What? What did Dad say?

Edward I suppose he hinted . . . he was implying . . . in a way he was saying that you made a choice.

Kyra looks at him a moment, then gets up to take the tea things out.

Look, whenever I mention it, he always says it's none of my business. He gets really angry. He says very little. I mean, I've been trying to get him to talk about you. Shit, that's what I mean, for fuck's sake. After all, it's my life as well. We saw you for years. Well, didn't we?

Kyra Yes. Yes, you did.

Edward Until just a few years ago. They were great times. Then you vanished. Why?

Kyra Think. Just think. It's probably the first thing you think of. And it's the reason.

She goes back into the kitchen area. Now Edward explodes, angry.

Edward And now are you saying I've no right to ask?

Kyra No.

Edward My mother died. She actually died. Not you. You did something else. You cut yourself off from us without saying anything. And in a way I'm coming to think that's much worse. Because you just left and said nothing. Alice had no choice. It wasn't her fault. But for you it's different. Because it's not necessary. Because yours is deliberate. And that makes it sort of more hurtful. I'm being hurt by someone for reasons they refuse to explain to me. And I'm left thinking . . . hang on, life is too short.

Kyra waits, still not answering, but he won't give up.

You know what it is? The thing that puzzles me, the thing I can't understand? It's odd, but it's true. Mum and Dad were much closer . . . they were always closer when you were there.

Kyra waits a moment, then answers quietly.

Kyra That's often true. Of a couple. They need a catalyst. A third person there, it helps them to talk.

Edward Is that all it was?

But this time it is Kyra who reacts as if it's at last too much.

Kyra Edward, come on, stop pushing me. This is a fight with your father. If you want to quarrel, then quarrel with him.

Edward is shocked by the reaction he has finally managed to provoke.

I'm glad you called round. I'm proud of you, Edward. You're a good boy. But you do seem to want to be judge and jury in some family court of your own making. And that's not the most attractive impulse to have.

Edward I'm sorry.

Kyra If you like judging, please: be a lawyer. Run a dog show. There's a whole lot of jobs if *judging* is your passion in life. But take my advice: if you want to be happy, keep your judging professional. And don't start putting in practice at home.

Both of them smile as she finishes her little speech. Now she goes to get one of her bags full of exercise books.

And now I'm afraid, I've a whole lot of homework . . .

Edward No, no, you're right. I've been really stupid.

Kyra No. Not at all.

Edward I was wondering . . .

Kyra What?

Edward At least . . . I've been wondering: what do you miss?

Kyra You mean, from your father's world?

Edward Yes.

Kyra stands in the middle of her shabby flat, mittens round her fingers, dreaming.

Kyra I miss a good breakfast. Toast wrapped in napkins. Croissants. And really hot coffee from a silver pot. Scrambled eggs. I never have those. And I do miss them more than I'd have thought possible.

Edward Nothing else?

Kyra Oh, maybe one thing. (*There is the shadow of a blush on her face.*)

Edward You miss my father.

For a moment it looks as if she does not know how to respond. Now it is Edward's turn to blush.

And so saying, I think I shall go.

Kyra has picked up his plastic bag and is holding it out to him.

Kyra Edward, I enjoyed seeing you. Really. I mean it.

Edward Right. Then I'm off.

Kyra You've got all your stuff?

Edward Yes. Yes, thank you.

He still seems rooted to the spot, even with his bag in his hand. She reaches forward and kisses him on the cheek.

I expect I'll see you again.

Kyra Yes, well, I hope so.

Edward You didn't mind?

Kyra Edward, I've said so.

He has run out of ways to prolong his departure. So impulsively he blurts out his last instruction.

Edward Kyra, I wish you would bloody well help.

And he turns and leaves as fast as he can. Kyra is slightly shaken for a moment, then she goes to the open door and closes it. She thinks a moment, then she goes out to the bathroom. After a second, the Ascot flares again, and there is the sound of a running bath. The lights fade.

SCENE TWO

*The lights come up again. In the kitchen the ingredients of
the spaghetti sauce have been laid out – onions, garlic and
chilli, none of them yet chopped. On the table the
schoolbooks have been laid out for an evening's reading.
After a moment there is a ringing at the door. Then a second
ringing and the sound of Kyra getting out of the bath.*

Kyra (*off*) Shit! (*As she comes into the room, wrapped in a
large towel and dripping wet, the ringing becomes more
insistent.*) Shit! Who is it? (*She goes into the kitchen and
looks down from the only window which gives on to the
street. She responds instinctively, without thinking.*) Jesus
Christ! Shit! Go away. (*The bell rings again. At once she
opens the window and calls down.*) Hold on a minute and
I'll throw down a key.

> *She takes a key which hangs on a hook in the kitchen and
> throws it out the window. She waits a moment to check
> it's been caught, then closes the window. She is panicking
> slightly. She goes into her bedroom, having collected
> jeans and a couple of sweaters. She goes across to the
> main door and opens it, then runs quickly back into the
> bathroom and closes the door.*
> *After a moment,* **Tom Sergeant** *appears in the
> doorway. He is near fifty, a big man, still with a lot of
> grey hair. He wears beautiful casual clothes under a coat.
> He has an air of slightly tired distinction. He stands a
> moment, looking round the room, but very quickly Kyra
> reappears in her jeans and sweater, her hair wet and a
> towel still in her hand.*

Kyra I wanted to say I'm not guilty.

Tom Not guilty? What do you mean?

Kyra You arrived like a fucking stormtrooper.

15

Tom Thank you.

Kyra Have you parked your tanks in the street?

Tom I was only ringing the bell.

She passes him to close the door, her tone dry.

Kyra You always were excessively manly.

Tom I brought you some whisky.

Kyra Thanks. Put it down over there.

Tom OK.

Kyra Beside the beer.

Tom frowns, seeing there is already a carrier bag full of beer on the table. Kyra passes back across the room, drying her hair.

Did somebody tell you? That if you called I'd be in?

Tom No. I was just guessing.

Kyra Oh really? Just passing?

Tom I wouldn't say that. I mean, does anyone . . .

Kyra Pass through this area? No. You've got a good point there. You mean this visit's deliberate?

Tom Yes. Sort of.

There is a moment's silence.

So.

Kyra Will you take off your coat?

Tom I won't. Just at this moment. Perhaps it's me. But it seems a bit parky.

Kyra It is.

Tom Well . . . I thought it was time. That's what I'm doing here. Time you and I saw each other again.

Kyra heads towards the kitchen. Tom starts wandering round the little flat.

Oh, I see you're making your supper. I'm sorry. Perhaps I should have phoned. I think I was scared you might hang up on me. I mean, I've had no idea. I mean, what you've been thinking. I suppose I thought perhaps you hated me.

Kyra Yes. If you'd rung then you'd have found out.

Tom nods slightly, recognizing and loving the old acerbity in her.

Tom It's not been easy. One way and another. It's been a hard time for me.

Kyra I heard about Alice.

Tom Did you? How?

Kyra I just heard.

Tom Yes. She died a year ago. It seems much longer. I mean, in a way it was fine. I'd already 'discounted' it. It's a term we use in business. Meaning . . .

Kyra I know what it means. You've already prepared yourself. So when it happens it isn't so awful.

Tom That's right. Yes. You're shocked?

Kyra Not at all. Should I be?

Tom No. Well, that's how it was.

He starts to move round the room correcting his apparent callousness.

And also Alice was so incredible. I can hardly tell you. I mean, she was so brave. Propped up in bed, wearing yellow.

She spent the day watching birds, through this large square of light above her. The skylight over her bed. She was truly . . . truly fantastic.

Kyra Whisky?

She is standing with the bottle poised over the glass. He catches her tone which seems unimpressed by his eulogy.

Tom Yes.

Kyra pours in silence. He looks at the CDs on the table.

Kyra, I must say you always surprise me. I'd never have thought you'd have taken up rap.

Kyra Oh. No, well, I haven't. In fact only recently.

Tom You know that Edward's into this stuff?

Kyra Oh really?

Tom Who are your favourites?

Kyra Oh. You know. It varies.

Tom I suppose you picked it up from your kids.

Kyra Sure.

Tom You're still at that same place?

Kyra Yeah.

Tom How is it?

Kyra At the moment? It's doing fine. I mean, we had a not-bad head teacher, truly she really wasn't too bad, but then – it always happens – things started wearing her down. (*She has got a bottle of red wine and has begun to open it.*) People started stealing her car. It was sort of a challenge or something. We think it must have been some of the kids. Then they broke into her flat. She lost her stereo. Also they got hold of her cat. She came back one night. The cat had

18

been baked in the oven. She began to feel it was time to move on. She got a better job, you know, down in Dulwich.

Tom Dulwich is nicer.

Kyra Yes, I think she probably felt that as well.

She looks at him witheringly, but he is imperturbable now.

Tom And what about you?

Kyra Me?

Tom Don't you get tired of it?

Kyra I talk to the police occasionally. They say it's a problem. Assaults on the police are growing all the time. Then they say, on the other hand, there's one thing they can't help noticing. It's the same coppers who get beaten up time and again.

Tom smiles, relaxed now with his whisky, as she goes to get herself a wine glass.

Tom So what does that mean?

Kyra Some people are victims. I walk in perfect peace to and from school. I'm not a mark, that's the difference.

Tom And what do you put that down to?

Instead of answering Kyra suddenly looks him straight in the eye and raises her voice.

Kyra I wish you'd take off your fucking coat.

Her directness suddenly speaks of a whole past between them. Tom replies quietly.

Tom Well, I would. Of course. If you'd get central heating. Then of course I'd take off my coat. But since you've made a style choice to live in Outer Siberia, I think for the moment I'll keep my coat on.

They are like old friends now as she pours herself a glass of wine.

If you want central heating, look, it's no problem. I've got this really good bloke.

Kyra From *Yellow Pages?*

Tom I'm sorry?

Kyra No, nothing.

Tom If you like, he'd come round. It wouldn't take long. This bloke does all of my restaurants. I'm pretty sure I can spare him next week. Unless of course you say, no thank you. I mean, no doubt you'd prefer to be cold.

Kyra No, I'd prefer to be warm.

Tom Well then.

Kyra Warm, but not indebted. If it's all right, I'm going to cook.

Tom Oh really? I was going to ask if you'd like proper dinner.

Kyra Meaning mine isn't proper? Spaghetti!

Tom Oh Lord, so touchy! No I meant, would you like to go out?

Kyra looks at him as if the question were absurd.

I'm just asking if you'd like to go out.

Kyra What for?

Tom An evening.

Kyra Tom, don't you think I've got enough memories? Why should I want any more?

She goes back to the cooking.

So tell me, how is the business?

Tom (*still refusing to be downhearted*) Business? Business has generally recovered. Yes, I'd even say it was thriving. Of course I'm not my own boss any more. In theory. Like everyone, I now have a chairman. The chairman of course has a bloody great board. That's the price I paid for going public. I report to this sort of management guru.

Kyra (*grimacing as she comes out opening a tin of tomatoes*) My God!

Tom I know, but, like all really top-class management gurus, he only comes in for four hours a week. He wanders in. Makes a few gnomic statements. Mutters the words 'core competence'. Or whatever trendy management mantra happens to be in fashion this week. Then he wanders out. For that the banks just love him. They adore him. Why? Because he once was a banker himself. So for this insider's sinecure he is paid more or less twice what I am paid as full-time chief executive. The person who created the company. The person who knows the business of hotels and restaurants. But that is the way that things are now done . . . (*He swirls the scotch in his glass.*)

Kyra What's he like?

Tom He's one of those people who's been told he's good with people. That means he smiles all the time and is terribly interested. He keeps saying 'No, tell me what do *you* think?'

Kyra In other words . . .

Tom Yes, he's completely insufferable.

Kyra is beginning to enjoy him now.

It was how I was always told you could get women into

bed. By doing something called 'listening to their problems'. It's a contemptible tactic.

Kyra You wouldn't do it?

Tom No. Of course not. You know me, Kyra. I wouldn't stoop to it. Listening's half way to begging. Either they want you or else they don't.

Kyra smiles as she goes to get a chopping board with which she comes back.

But this bloke . . . he does it all the time in the business. 'How interesting. Really? Is that what you think?' Then he does what he'd planned in the first place. It's called consultation. Buttering you up and then ignoring you.

Kyra (*setting down the board*) I can imagine.

Tom Oh yes, that's how things go nowadays . . .

Kyra Is there no way you can get rid of him?

Tom No. It's the price I paid for floating the company. It made me millions, I can hardly complain. I offered you shares, remember? I never knew why you refused.

Kyra flashes a look at him to suggest he knows perfectly well why she refused.

When we went public they jumped thirty-fold. You could have had the house in the West Indies. Like me.

Kyra Oh, really?

Tom Well maybe not quite. But at least you could have moved up in the world.

Kyra ignores this, choosing to go on chopping the onions.

Banks and lawyers! That's all I see. So perhaps you did well. Perhaps it wasn't so stupid. Coming here.

Kyra It wasn't stupid.

Tom No.

She has spoken with such quiet firmness that he looks up. Then he moves away, implicitly accepting what she's just said, but happy to resume his stories.

Me, I'm with shits and shafters all day. I went in to one guy, the other day, I said to this fellow – he's lending me money at eleven per cent – I said: 'You want it? Well you can have it. You want the shirt off my back? I will hand you my shirt. Here it is! And still, as God is my witness, you will not stop me, you will not stop me from trying to build a business out there.' (*He stands now, re-creating the moment.*) I said, 'I'm an entrepreneur, I'm a doer. I actually go out, I make things happen. I give people jobs which did not previously exist. And you . . . you sit here with your little piles of money. Doing fuck all.'

Kyra How did he take it?

Tom Oh, no problem! The odd thing was, he agreed. (*Tom is in his stride, the raconteur happy with his favourite audience.*) He said, 'Yes of course, you're right, that's right. It's true. You take the risks and I never do. I hate risks!' he said. 'But also,' he said, 'has it occurred to you that this may be the reason finally why it's *you* who always has to come grovelling to *me*?'

Kyra He didn't say 'grovelling'?

Tom (*suddenly exasperated*) Kyra, there's nothing more irritating . . .

Kyra All right, I'm sorry . . .

Tom No, Alice . . . Alice would do this. I would say, I'm telling a story. For God's sake I'm telling a story. If I say it, it's true.

Kyra I know.

Tom 'Oh, I don't believe it,' Alice would say . . . (*He is more emphatic than ever, as if mystified why anyone would doubt him.*) I wouldn't say it if it wasn't what happened. *I wouldn't say it!*

Kyra I know.

Tom That's what he said to me!

Kyra He used the word 'grovelling'?

Tom Those exact words! 'And that is why you come grovelling to me . . .'

> *Kyra laughs again, now Tom is back on track, his humour restored.*

Kyra Well I must say . . . who was he?

Tom Some fucking graduate in business studies. Twenty-five. Thirty. Knows nothing. The Rolex! The fucking lemon-yellow Gaultier tie!

Kyra Goodness, the banks have got trendy.

Tom They're beyond trendy. The banks are running the world. You think – oh fuck! – you think, I'll run a business, I'll build a business. You remember, Kyra, we started out, my God it was great! Actually counting the money, you counted it with me . . .

Kyra Of course.

Tom Actually handling the money each morning, after you'd joined us, totting it up each Saturday night . . .

Kyra I remember.

Tom Then – oh Christ! – there's this fatal moment. Expansion!

Kyra Sure.

Tom And then you borrow. And then you're no longer in business, you're no longer in what I'd call business, because it's nothing to do with the customer. It's you and the bank. And it's war! (*He stops, incisive.*) There was a moment, I tell you, in the middle eighties . . .

Kyra Oh yeah . . .

Tom Yeah, just for a moment, I tell you, there was a time. I think, through that little window – what was it? Four years? Five years? Just through that little opening in history you could feel the current. For once you could feel the current running your way. You walked into a bank, you went in there, you had an idea. In. Money. Thank you. Out. Bang! They gave you the money! It was like for a moment we all had a vision, it was a kind of a heavenly vision, the idea of how damn fast and fun it could be . . . (*He turns, whisky in hand.*) And then of course everything slipped back to normal. The old 'are you sure that's what you really want to do?' The 'wouldn't it be easier if we all did nothing at all?' They always have new ways of punishing initiative. Whatever you do, they think up new ways.

Kyra looks up a moment, but Tom is already going on to tell her more.

You know, you read all this stuff in the papers – this stuff about banks – you read it, you know what I mean . . .

Kyra No. I'm afraid I've stopped reading the papers.

Tom What are you saying? Not altogether?

Tom is taken aback, but Kyra is going on, amused at her own story.

Kyra It's funny, I remember my father. Dad used to say, 'I don't watch the news. I don't approve of it.' I used to say,

'Dad, it's the news. It's the *news*, for God's sake. How can you not *approve* of it?' But I must say, now . . . perhaps I'm my father's daughter . . . I tend to think that he had a point. I don't have a television either.

Tom But that is just crazy. You're . . .

Kyra What?

Tom Well, you're missing what's happening. You're missing reality.

Kyra Oh, do you think?

> *Even Tom is only half-serious, knowing his argument doesn't sound too good. And Kyra is completely unfazed.*

I just noticed the papers were full of . . . sort of unlikeable people. People I couldn't relate to. People who weren't like the decent people, the regular people I meet every day at the school. So I thought, I start reading this stuff and half an hour later, I wind up angry. So perhaps it's better I give it up.

Tom So what do you read?

Kyra On the bus I read classic novels. Computer manuals. It's like that game. Name a politician you actually admire. So what is the point of sitting there raging at all the insanity?

Tom That's not the point.

Kyra It's the same with new films. I just won't go to them. Old films I like.

Tom Ah. Those you like because they're romantic.

Kyra You can hardly deny it. They have something we don't.

> *Suddenly her words hang in the air between them.*

Almost to cover the embarrassment, she resumes.

And Edward?

Tom What?

Kyra How is Edward?

Tom looks at her blankly as if not knowing who she's talking about.

Kyra Edward. Edward, your son?

Tom Oh bloody Edward, that's who you mean. He's fine. I mean, he's living. He's alive. I mean, he gives the external signs. He eats. He tries to spend all my money. What can you say except he's eighteen? (*Before Kyra can react, Tom is off again, on a half-serious complaint.*) I saw that old film. *Invasion of the Body Snatchers.* You know, where they look the same. They look like humans, but it turns out they're creatures from Mars. They're pods. Well, another way of putting it, they're male adolescents. It's like they get taken over. Someone comes and surgically removes all the good qualities they have, and turns them into selfish hoodlums . . .

Kyra I don't believe it's really that bad.

Kyra picks up the board and takes it out to the kitchen. Tom has already moved away to pour himself a second scotch.

Tom I mean, you spend all this money on education. A generation builds something up. And the children learn nothing but how to stand back from it . . .

Kyra Tom, that is nonsense.

Tom And all they want is to knock everything down.

Kyra reaches now for a frying pan, not thinking he's serious. But he shakes his head, bitter, his indignation now real.

27

He called me a brainless animal.

Kyra No? Really? That's unspeakable.

Tom That's what he called me. Buying and selling. That's what he said. Without ever questioning. He called me a zombie . . .

Kyra No!

Tom Just doing business without asking why . . . (*He doesn't see her quiet amusement at this story as he reaches past her to pour water into his scotch from the tap.*) I said, perhaps it's true, perhaps I'm not brilliantly contemplative, perhaps I do not stop like some Oxford smartarse philosopher to ask myself the purpose of it all. But the rough effect of all my endeavour – my putting my house, my mortgage, my car, the whole of my bloody life on the line – as I reminded him *I have done in my time* – has been to embody this unspeakably crude assumption that it's still worth human beings trying to get something done . . . (*He has landed on this last phrase, getting pleasure now from his own rhetoric.*)

Kyra And what did he say?

Tom Say? *Say?* You mean, like 'say' as in the concept of actually replying? Kyra, you don't understand. This is the modern game. This is men's tennis. People don't bother with rallies. You put in your big serve and you hope to hell it never comes back. (*Tom turns, expansive, bitter.*) He's not like what you'd call rational-articulate. He doesn't want argument. For Christ's sake, Kyra, you teach. Language belongs to the past. This is the world of Super-Mario. Bang! Splat! Spit out your venom and go. (*He looks at her, his tone softening now.*) It's not like, you know . . . when we were together. You and me talking. Talking down the stars from the sky. This is . . . oh you know . . . it's instinct. This is a young man wanting to hurt.

Kyra And does he hurt?

Tom No, of course not. For God's sake, look, I've fought bigger than him. He can't get a glove on me. That's why he's angry. (*He is aware that Kyra thinks his bravado sounds a little unconvincing. So he moves away a few paces.*) There's no problem. It's all in hand.

> *Kyra nods. It has gone quiet. Both of them know he is not telling the truth. He has gone to the kitchen door and now watches as she pours the olive oil into the frying pan. She looks at him as she works because he is standing so close.*

Kyra What? No, really. What are you thinking?

Tom Are you putting the chilli in first?

> *Kyra looks at him uncharitably. He is at his most boyish, hesitant.*

No, it's just I usually . . . I fry the chilli, so it infuses the oil.

Kyra Uh-huh. I see. I don't do that. I'm doing it the way I prefer.

Tom Yeah. (*He shifts a moment, uneasy.*) I haven't quite asked you. I mean, if I'm going to stay. I mean . . . I just mean for supper. I'm actually asking. I mean, are you laying two plates?

> *In reply she takes plates from the rack and goes to the table at which she has been meaning to work. She clears the books to one side. Then she puts two plates down at opposite ends of the table. Then she goes back to the kitchen and resumes. All in silence. He makes a little bow.*

Thank you. Believe me, I'm really grateful.

Kyra Think nothing of it.

Tom Oh, and put the chilli in first.

Kyra gives him a filthy look, but he is already out of range, relaxing again.

You never cooked.

Kyra No, I didn't.

Tom I remember in those early days once you asking if you could try it some time . . .

Kyra I never did. I was a happy waitress.

Tom You weren't a waitress for long.

Kyra I was a waitress for forty-five minutes. Alice made me the boss on the spot.

Tom is happily shaking his head at the memory, as Kyra now cooks.

Tom That was a night.

Kyra It was.

Tom Hilary's accident!

Kyra It was my first trip to London, I just walked in off the street . . .

Tom You were eighteen.

Kyra Incredible!

Tom You were the same age Edward is now.

Kyra I was so thrilled, I remember. At last I'd escaped. I was walking down London's famous King's Road. I saw the sign 'Waitress Wanted'. I walked in. Alice told me I could start right away. Then after an hour of it, she came running over. She said her daughter was in hospital, she'd fallen off her bike. She said she'd looked round and she'd decided. Could I run the place for the night?

Tom laughs at the ridiculousness of it. Kyra has stopped at the frying pan.

I said, 'I've only just started, I only started an hour ago.' She said, 'I know. I've watched you. I trust you. Now you must trust me, you're going to be fine . . .'

Tom What time was that? Do you remember?

Kyra Oh it can't have been later than eight o'clock.

Tom Before the rush?

Kyra I mean, oh yes. I handled it. I know I did the whole thing. Then I closed up. All the waiters were great, they were great considering I'd only just arrived yet I was in charge. They all said, 'Look, we promise, there's really no need for you to hang on here. Just lock up the door and we're all going home . . .' (*She has left the cooking, and is now standing at the kitchen door.*) But I don't know . . . I just had this instinct. Somehow I didn't think it was right. I can't quite explain it. I wanted to be there when Alice got back. It's funny. Of course, I would have met you anyway. Surely I would have met you next day. Who knows? But there was something about that evening. Something to do with the evening itself . . .

She looks away absently. Tom has sat down and is rapt.

I sat alone. Drank espresso. Smoked cigarettes. I'm not sure I'd ever sat through a night. This deserted restaurant all to myself. But filled with inexpressible happiness. This crazy feeling. 'I don't know why but this is where I belong.'

Tom And then?

Kyra And then . . . Need I continue? Then towards morning she came back with you.

Kyra turns and goes back to work. For the first time Tom is at peace.

Tom Earlier she'd rung. I'd driven like a madman from some meeting. In those days I had the Jag. Praying. Weeping. You know, feeling not like myself, because I thought. . . I was thinking, I'm not a person who cries. Crying with relief, too, at the sight of Hilary. Fast asleep in the little bed. Her leg in plaster. Some fucking nurse. What terrible parents! How could you let your daughter play in the road?

Kyra has stirred her pan and now is listening to him at the kitchen door.

Then, when we came back, you brought us brandy and coffee. In our own restaurant. At four o'clock. It was completely natural. I thought, this is the strangest night of my life. This girl I'd never met before, bringing brandy and coffee. It's as if she's been with us the whole of our lives.

Kyra looks down, moved by this.

Yeah, that was something.

Kyra It was.

Tom Didn't you stay with us?

Kyra I did. I stayed at your place. On the floor. Well, I have to say that was my moment. From that moment on . . . I'd have done anything, just to stay with you, just to stay in that house.

She goes back to the cooking.

Tom I remember I got really angry soon after, after a few weeks or so, you saying you weren't going to give up a place at university. You weren't going to make your life in the catering trade.

Kyra I didn't say 'catering'! I never used the words 'catering trade'! Honestly, you make me sound like a prig.

Tom No? A prig? Impossible! You're a seaside solicitor's daughter! Are you saying that some of that hadn't rubbed off?

Kyra has picked up her glass of red wine, laughing at his account. At last, she is unguarded.

Kyra It's just . . . for goodness' sake . . . I loved mathematics. I did. I loved it. I wasn't going to give up half way. And what's more, it meant finally escaping my father. I was hardly going to pass up that chance.

Tom shrugs, unimpressed.

It wasn't easy. You started to lecture me. I was quite shocked. 'Don't waste your time on higher education, it's only a way of postponing real life . . .'

Tom So it is.

Kyra I was so worried, I went to Alice. I said, 'Does he mean it? She said, 'Never take any notice of Tom . . .'

Tom Thank you, Alice . . .

Kyra 'And even if you go, he knows you'll always want to come back . . .' (*She looks at him, serious now, the words etched out, sincere.*) You gave me a place. It was there. I could count on your welcome.

There is a slight pause, Tom moved by Kyra's acknowledgement of how much their home had meant to her.

And I never doubted, not for a moment, that when I came back to London, there'd be a job waiting.

She stops a second. Then a real mischievousness comes into her manner.

In spite of – my God! – whatever else I was doing. Far more, let me tell you, far more than you ever knew. . . .

Tom Yes, well, I have to say I assumed, I hardly thought – you were young enough, for God's sake – I hardly thought you lived the life of a nun.

Kyra You wish!

Tom You thought I was jealous?

Kyra You did tear that painting from the wall.

Tom I did not tear it. As God is my witness, I did not remove it. It fell.

Kyra Oh yes, I see, pure coincidence, this picture painted by a man of whom you happened not to approve . . .

Tom Colin! The original art-school wanker . . . the greasy beard and the clogs . . .

Kyra Who had painted me at college, as I felt rather beautifully . . .

Tom Rather beautifully, but wearing no clothes.

Kyra That was the point. You could not stand it. You saw me there on the wall.

Tom It's true. I looked at it. I just looked at it. I sent beams of hatred from across the room. And without my touching it, I admit it fell down.

Kyra Oh, sure.

She turns and goes back into the kitchen to put the spaghetti into boiling water.

Tom (*defending himself, half serious, half not*) It wasn't – be fair! – it wasn't the sight of you, it wasn't just the image of you, it was my disbelief . . . my horror that this young woman who seemed so capable . . . so smart . . .

Kyra Thank you . . .

Tom . . . should have had the clothes ripped off her as if they were tissue as soon as some phoney used the word 'art'. (*He sums up his charges as she cooks on.*) I thought you were gullible!

Kyra No, I was open-minded. And what's more, twenty years younger than you. And living a life. You actually tried to give me a lecture . . .

Tom is about to deny it.

You did! You said, 'In a way you're part of the family, in a way, Kyra, you're like a daughter of mine . . .'

Tom I didn't say 'daughter'!

Kyra Oh, but you did.

Tom Where was this?

Kyra That ghastly hamburger restaurant you had. You were in your chargrilled hamburger phase.

Tom Oh God, I'm ashamed! I mean, I'm ashamed of the lecture, I'm ashamed of those burgers as well.

Kyra (*suddenly shouting as if there is no end to the awfulness of it all*) The burgers! The lecture!

Tom I must say, it begins to come back . . .

Kyra And I thought, yes, oh I see. I realized then: Here we go.

Tom What?

Kyra I thought, hold on. This is it. This is only going to be a matter of time.

She has come back into the room and finds herself standing right by his chair, close enough to touch. The contact is now so intimate between them that it suddenly feels as if either of them might say anything. Then Tom speaks as if the next thought were completely logical.

Tom *Pressing on.* You know, that's the thing in business. My chairman keeps telling me: never look back. In business, he says, the world was created this morning. No such thing as the past . . .

Kyra turns to go and look after her pasta.

He says that modern management asks you to look at your assets, *really* look at them – this is a fierce, competitive world, all that crap! – how you got here's not part of the story, the only story is what you do now . . .

Kyra And what do you do?

Tom Oh, expand, inevitably. I mean, expand, I hardly need say that. Defend market share. Build another stainless steel restaurant, this one larger, more fashionable than ever, turning over hundreds of covers in a day. It need never end.

Kyra Nor will it. You love it.

Tom Oh yes. I must admit that I do. (*He looks at her, on safe ground, the feeling once more easy and warm.*) All that time, I must say, I can't deny it, while Alice was . . . you know . . . while she was lying in that bloody room . . . well, it was true for me, I saw no alternative but to redouble my efforts. It was like some lunatic board game. Not helped of course by your having quit.

He looks at her a little sheepishly.

It's true, though, I must say I missed you professionally.

Kyra Thank you.

They both know this thought is incomplete and how it will be, in a moment, completed.

Tom I kind of missed you in person as well.

36

Kyra looks at him a moment, just non-committal as she works. Tom is serious.

I really did, Kyra. I never . . . I've never got used to it. Ever.

Kyra What, missed me so badly, it's taken you three years to get back in touch?

It is said lightly, Kyra not wanting the atmosphere to darken, but he at once starts to protest strongly.

Tom Now look . . .

Kyra I mean, come on, let's be serious . . .

Tom You think I haven't wanted to? My God, you think I haven't wanted to call? To pick up the telephone? You think I haven't wanted to jump in the car and bust my way through that bloody door?

Kyra But then why didn't you?

Tom Kyra, why do you think?

They both know a bridge is about to be crossed even before it happens.

Because I knew once I saw you, then I'd be finished. I knew I'd never be able to leave.

He is so clearly speaking from the heart that Kyra cannot say anything. So instead she turns and goes back to her pasta.

Kyra OK, well, I must say, that's an answer . . .

Tom You see.

Kyra What?

Tom I'm getting better. Well, aren't I?

Kyra Getting better at what?

Tom Talking about my feelings. You always told me I had no gift for that stuff.

She frowns, puzzled at this.

Kyra As far as I remember we had no need for it. We had no need to discuss our feelings at all. Or rather, I didn't. I could always tell what you were feeling. It never had to be said. You'd wander about the office in Chelsea. Later we'd go home to work. We'd sit in the kitchen with Alice. I'd spend the evening reading to your kids.

There is a moment's silence. Tom is serious, low, when he speaks.

Tom I could never understand it. I still don't. You never felt the slightest sense of betrayal.

Kyra There we are. I always felt profoundly at peace. (*She waits a moment, wanting to be precise.*) I don't know why, it still seems true to me: if you have a love, which for any reason you can't talk about, your heart is with someone you can't admit – not to a single soul except for the person involved – then for me, well, I have to say, that's love at its purest. For as long as it lasts, it's this astonishing achievement. Because it's always a relationship founded in trust.

Tom It seems mad to me.

Kyra I know. You didn't feel that. I knew you never understood it. Why I was able to go on seeing Alice. Why we were always at ease. Why I loved her so much. But I did. It's a fact. There it is. The three of us. It gave me a feeling of calm. (*She has got a small lump of cheese in greaseproof paper out of the fridge, and a cheese grater, and is coming back into the room.*) You were the person I fell in love with. And as it happened you arrived with a wife.

Tom stands unimpressed by her argument, and rather hurt by her cheerfulness about it all. Kyra holds the cheese out to him.

Do you mind?

Tom Do I mind what?

Kyra No, I'm just asking . . .

Tom What?

Kyra I'm asking. Will you grate the cheese?

Tom takes the sweaty piece of greaseproof paper from her and holds it in his hand.

Tom Do you mean this?

Kyra I do.

Tom Are you serious? Is this what you're calling the cheese?

Nonchalant, she smiles and goes back to the kitchen as he moves, genuinely affronted by the cheese in his hand.

Kyra Yeah, I haven't had time to go shopping.

Tom I wouldn't give this greasy lump of crud to my cat.

Tom is holding out this piece of cheese somehow to represent the final insanity of her way of life. He raises his voice as if everything has become too much for him.

I do not believe it. Kyra, what's happening? Are you really *living* like this? Why didn't you say? For God's sake, I have this supplier . . .

Kyra I'm sure!

Tom For cheese – all types of cheese – I have this really great bloke.

Kyra Of course! Your whole life is great blokes!

Tom I mean, I can get you a weekly delivery – no problem – he'll send you fresh parmesan whenever you need.

Kyra Nevertheless.

She nods at the cheese in his hand to say he has no choice. But Tom already has another plan.

Tom I'm going to get Frank.

Kyra I'm sorry?

Tom I'm going to call down to Frank, this is ridiculous, to send out, just to go to a deli and get us something for now . . .

Kyra Hold on a moment, what are you saying? Are you saying that Frank is sitting out there?

Tom Sure.

Kyra Waiting out in the car all the time we've been talking?

Tom Yes. I mean, yes! For Christ's sake, what's wrong with that?

He is bemused but she has her hands on her hips, as if Tom will never learn.

Kyra You leave him down there? You really are quite extraordinary.

Tom Why?

Kyra You used to tell me you had this great gift! I remember, you prided yourself on what you called your man-management skills. And yet you still treat people as if they were no better than objects . . .

But Tom is already moving in to her, refusing to accept any of this.

Tom For God's sake, Kyra, the man is a driver. That's what he does. You know full well that drivers don't drive. The greater part of their lives they spend waiting . . .

Kyra Tom, there is some sort of limit!

Tom And furthermore, that is what they expect. Frank, I may tell you . . . Frank, as it happens, is perfectly happy. Frank for a start is bloody well paid. He is sitting in a spacious limousine listening to Kiss 100 and reading what is politely called a 'men's interest' magazine . . .

But Kyra is already pointing to the window in the kitchen area.

Kyra Have you looked out the window? Have you seen the weather? Have you seen there's snow about to come down?

Tom Don't give me that tosh! Frank is a bloody sight better off sitting in a warm Mercedes than he would be in this fucking fur-store which you call your home.

Kyra Well . . .

Tom (*suddenly exploding with rage*) I mean here we are! This is the problem! That's what it was. That was the problem. This ridiculous self-righteousness! I mean, to be fair, you always had it. But also, I knew, I *knew* it wasn't going to get better. And, let's face it, it was only going to get worse once you decided you wanted to teach.

Kyra It's nothing to do with my teaching, it isn't to do with the work that I do, it's just a way of respecting people.

Tom Frank isn't people! Frank is a man who is doing a job! (*He moves away, all his worst suspicions confirmed.*) You were always salving your own bloody conscience . . . these stupid gestures, nothing to do with what people might want. They want to be treated . . . respected like adults for the job they are paid for, and not looked down on as if they were chronically disabled, as if they somehow need *help* all the time. I mean, yes, this was the craziness! This was the whole trouble with business and you! You looked down – always! – on the way we did things. The way things are done. You could never accept the nature of business. I mean, finally that's why you had to leave.

He has no sooner said this than he realizes how absurd it is, and at once tries to retract.

Kyra Well I must say . . .

Tom I mean . . .

Kyra I never knew that was the reason!

Tom All right, I'm sorry . . .

Kyra I never knew that was why I had to leave.

Tom is desperately trying to backtrack but Kyra won't let him off the hook.

Tom I put it badly.

Kyra Badly? You did. I thought I left because your wife discovered I'd been sleeping with you for over six years!

Unable to resist it, she has said this so forcefully that he can only look at her, admitting his own absurdity.

Tom I mean, well, yes. That as well, that played a part in it.

Kyra I should say it fucking well did.

Tom That was part of the problem.

Kyra Part of? *Part* of?

Tom But you did have a problem of attitude. Your attitude to business you never got straight!

Kyra Well . . .

She gestures as if this was hardly the worst of her

*problems and goes back into the kitchen to carry on
laying the table.*

Tom (*trying to retrieve what ground he can*) What I'm
saying is, you'd have left anyway. I could sense it. You were
feeling it was time for a change.

Kyra Tom, I left because I'd always warned you: 'If Alice
finds out, then I shall go.'

*She has said this quite simply as if re-creating the
moment. Tom shifts, uncomfortable, more like a little
boy than ever.*

Tom All right . . .

Kyra I told you, I told you a thousand times . . .

Tom Yes. I know you did.

Kyra I can only do this for as long as she doesn't find out.
When she found out, then it changed things. Instantly.

Tom 'Instantly' says it. You were gone in an hour. Wham!
Out the door! With me left explaining to all the other
employees . . .

Kyra Oh, really?

Tom I don't think anyone was very convinced.

Kyra I had no choice. I know it sounds stupid. You have
something worked out in your own mind. Then something
changes. The balance is gone. You no longer believe your
own story. And that, I'm afraid, is the moment to leave.

*She turns and goes out into the kitchen. Tom moves
away, thinking, by himself. He picks up the cheese and
the grater and, as if conceding defeat, starts to grate it
into a little bowl. Kyra speaks quietly from the kitchen.*

Kyra I heard you moved.

43

Tom Yes. We did that quite quickly. We moved when Alice was starting to get ill.

Kyra How long was her illness?

Tom She was . . . well, let's see . . . she was in the bed, in the bad bit, I suppose, it was getting on for a year. I mean we'd known, I mean soon after you left us . . . then she began to experience dizziness. She'd taken no notice at first.

Kyra has stopped cooking, and is just watching him now.

We were in such total confusion, at that time things were already so tough, so that news of the illness . . . to be honest, at first, when it was first diagnosed, it seemed like kind of a joke. How much misfortune? and so on. Where are the gods?

Kyra just watches, not reacting. The cheese and grater are idle in his hands.

She needed a place where she could be peaceful. I built this extraordinary bedroom – this builder, the one I mentioned, you know – with this wonderful sloping glass roof. The Common outside. Fantastic! We gave her the picture she wanted, exactly what she wanted to see. (*Then he frowns, knowing what he will say next is difficult.*) She became quite . . . well, she became quite mystic. I don't mean to sound cruel but it was kind of difficult for me.

Kyra In what way?

Tom You know Alice. She got hold of this bloody word 'spiritual'. It's one of those words I've never quite understood. I mean, I've always hated the way people use it. They use it to try and bump themselves up. 'Oh I've had a spiritual experience,' they say . . .

Kyra Yes.

Tom As if that's the end of the argument. Spiritual, meaning: 'it's mine and shove off.' People use it to prove they're sensitive. They want it to dignify quite ordinary things. (*Tom has started by half-sending himself up but now he gets firmer as he goes.*) Religion. Now, that is something different. I like religion. Because religion has rules. It's based on something which actually occurred. There are things to believe in. And what's more, what makes it worth following – not that I do, mind you – there's some expectation of how you're meant to behave. But 'spiritual' . . . well, it's all wishy-washy. It means 'well for me, for *me* this is terribly important, but I'm fucked if I can really say why . . .'

Kyra is smiling at this characteristic talk, but Tom is genuinely aggravated.

Kyra Is that how Alice was?

Tom Oh look, I don't mean to downgrade it. Alice was dying. Let's face it, in my view, she grabbed at whatever she could. She was always faddish. But that's what it was. Grabbing. It wasn't solid. It wasn't like she really believed. If you'd said, 'Oh look, what do you believe in? What is there? What's happening? What's real?', she couldn't say. It was all sensation.

Kyra is looking askance now, a little shocked by Tom's dismissiveness.

Kyra Yes, but Tom, surely, that's not so unusual . . .

Tom I know!

Kyra That's how most people die. They die in that state. Not knowing. Half knowing. Surely that's what you'd expect?

Tom (*turning round, determined again to confront his own unease*) I don't know. I could see the room was beautiful. I mean, it was a beautiful room. And so it should be. I'm not being wholly facetious, but the fact is I had spent a great deal. I mean, I'm not kidding. I spent a great deal of money. All that glass, the sandalwood floor. The sky! The greenery! The light! I gave her everything.

Kyra So what are you saying?

Tom I don't know. I just felt frustrated. I felt out of contact.

Kyra What you're saying is the two of you never got straight.

Tom No.

It is suddenly quiet. Kyra is standing with the cooking spoon still in her hand. Tom is just staring out. There is a feeling of shame and complicity. Briefly, they're like two criminals.

Kyra What you mean is you never got over your guilt.

She goes back towards the kitchen.

Tom (*quietly, a little hoarsely*) Guilt. I don't know. I mean, guilt's another word. It's one of those words people use. I mean, sure. In a way. I mean, yes, I can hardly deny it. Both of us knew. Both Alice and me. We knew our time together was wrecked. But Alice was far too proud to reproach me. And then of course, being Alice, she began to withdraw. Gardening! Sewing! Reading! All those feminine things! The effect? To make me feel much worse than if she'd stood up and fought.

Kyra is standing listening again now, recognizing his description of Alice.

She kept saying, 'No, you go on with your life, Tom. We're such different people,' that's what she said. 'Don't mind me. Forget me. I'm happy reading and gardening.' Christ! Fucking gardening! If I could make it illegal I would!

Kyra smiles.

She'd say quietly, 'Well, you know, Tom, I think we were always mismatched. For a man like you, Kyra is much more intelligent.' She'd praise you. Always. 'Kyra's attractive. She's clever. She's smart.' I mean she'd actually say that. 'I'm much too docile, I know.' Jesus! I look back on that time in our lives, my own wife telling me in tones of absolute sweetness how right I was to love someone else. And what's more, what a good choice! (*He turns back, despairing.*) Then when she got ill . . .you think, I see, is this some sort of punishment? Do You always punish the meek? Alice's peace of mind taken from her. Her friendship with you. She's just beginning to absorb this. And then she's told that she's going to die.

Kyra (*gently, curiously.*) And now?

Tom Now?

Kyra What are you feeling?

Tom looks at her blankly for a moment, then characteristically covers up again, at once trying to hide his distress.

Tom Oh, not too bad. I think I'm all right. No, really. I've found ways of coping. In the way that you do. I mean, I've got the business. No problem. I've got the house. (*Then he grins, relieved to be able to get back to an anecdote.*) A woman came – I didn't tell you this – a woman came to the door. She said she was from a local support group. I couldn't believe it. She told me she'd come to help me to grieve. I said, 'I beg your pardon?' She said, don't worry, it's not going to cost you. It's on the rates. Or the Poll Tax, whatever it's called. I said, 'I'm meant to feel better? You mean that's meant to make it all right? That's meant to make all the difference? Oh good, this is great, I think I'll do this, I'll mourn my wife in the company of this total

47

stranger, after all it's going to be *free* . . . (*Now he is becoming disproportionately angry, his scorn for his visitor complete.*) I said, 'Look, lady, I'll tell you one thing. When I choose to grieve for this woman . . . this woman with whom I spent such a . . . *large* part of my life, it will not be in the presence of a representative of Wimbledon Council.' She said, 'Oh we're in Merton now.'

He stands, genuinely furious, lost, all his anger displaced on to this story.

I mean, please tell me, what is it? Don't they know anything? You suffer. That's what you do. There are no short cuts. There are no easy ways. And I have been doing my share of suffering.

Kyra Yes. I know that. That's what I've heard.

Tom frowns, brought up short, suddenly hearing her say this.

Tom What do you mean? What do you mean by that?

Kyra I talked to Edward.

Tom Edward?

Kyra That's right.

Tom When? You've talked to Edward?

Kyra Oh shit, the pasta is going to be done . . .

She moves quickly to reach into the oven for the plates.

Tom (*infuriated*) For Christ's sake, forget the pasta.

Kyra Oh God, I think it's going to be spoilt.

Tom What are you saying? Have you kept on seeing Edward?

Kyra No. He's only been over here once.

48

Tom When?

Kyra As it happened, this evening. He came, he told me that you'd been impossible. He says you still can't live with yourself. He said you spend the whole day in a fury.

Tom Fury? What fury?

Kyra He says you're totally lost.

Tom How dare he? How dare he come here and talk about me?

But Kyra, pouring the water off the pasta, is catching some of Tom's anger.

Kyra He came out of kindness. He came because he's concerned for his father.

Tom Concerned? Concerned for his father? Like fuck! He came because he's a little shit-stirrer. Because he likes making other people's business his own.

Suddenly Kyra's patience goes. She picks up a tray of cutlery and throws it violently across the room. The crash is spectacular. Tom stands dazed.

Kyra This is it. I mean, *shit*! I've heard you, Tom . . . I mean you've done this, you've done this your whole bloody life . . .

Tom Done what?

Kyra Pretended not to understand anything. Pretended, when you understand perfectly well.

Tom Understand what?

Kyra You've taken this boy . . .

Tom I've *taken* him?

Kyra You've taken this son of yours. Edward. You've made his life miserable. He told me. You had a row. For God's sake, earlier this week, he left home.

Tom *So?*

Kyra You're making his life unendurable. And only because you happen to be so bloody guilty . . .

Tom Me?

Kyra And so you take your guilt out on him.

Tom Is that what I do?

Kyra It is.

Tom Oh, really?

Kyra Yes.

Tom I see. Is that his opinion?

Kyra I think so.

Tom Is that his *version*? Is that what he says?

Kyra He didn't need to say it. I lived with your family, remember? Do you think I don't know what the hell's going on?

> *Tom moves away again, happier now, hoping he's off the hook.*

Tom Ah, now I see, Kyra, you're actually inventing. I see. This is guesswork. The truth is, you're making this up. From your knowledge of the family you once walked out on . . .

Kyra All right . . .

Tom Edward didn't actually say any of this . . .

> *But she won't give way. She is still standing resolute, determined to take him on.*

Kyra I think he saw your behaviour.

Tom My behaviour?

Kyra The way you behaved at the end. (*She stops, knowing she has hit home.*) He was there. He knew your real feelings. And I think that's why you're punishing him now.

Tom just looks at her. Knowing it's true, she goes further on to the attack.

Do you think, please, Tom, do you think I've believed the lies you've been telling me?

Tom Lies?

Kyra Yes, of course. 'I'm enjoying the business, it's wonderful. I get on great with my son. Alice dying was hard, but of course I survived it. No problem. I just dropped round to see you . . . Oh, no reason, I just thought it was time . . .' (*She is bitter at the absurdity of it.*) And me, I'm standing here, nodding, smiling, agreeing like some ape . . . and thinking, is this man lying to me deliberately? Or does he not even notice? Or is he so used to lying to himself? It's all right for me. I'm fine. You can tell me anything. Any old story. I'm lucky because I've moved on. But Edward is young. He needs his father. He deserves honesty. He deserves not to be treated like dirt.

Tom looks guiltily at her a moment, not wanting to give way completely.

Tom That isn't fair.

Kyra Oh, isn't it?

Tom It isn't one-sided. Sometimes, I know, I can be hard on the boy.

Kyra And why?

Tom He's such a jerk. That's the reason.

He looks at her reproachfully a moment, then suddenly admits the truth.

All right, it's true. I couldn't face Alice. I couldn't. Not at the end. Any excuse. I went travelling. I opened hotels abroad. New York. Los Angeles. The further, the better. I couldn't – I know it was wrong of me – do you really think I don't know it? – but, Jesus . . . I could not stay in that room. All right, I'm not proud. We both knew what was happening. I kept thinking, it's not like a test. What's happening is chance. It's pure chance. It's simply bad luck. But I couldn't fight it. I felt . . . oh, everyone's watching. Her friends. I know what they think. This is some sort of trial of my character. And no doubt the bastards are saying I fail. (*He is suddenly vehement.*) But Edward was as bad. Don't ever think otherwise. He failed just as badly. In a different way. I came home, six friends of his lying on the floor, drinking Heineken. Drugs. Shit, I don't know . . . I remember screaming, 'What the hell are you doing? Don't you know your mother is lying up there?' I was so angry. I felt this anger, I never got over it. Every day this fury that you had walked out. Walked out and left me to handle this thing. I did try to use it. I used your memory. I kept saying, look, I must behave well. I must try. Because who knows? If I behave well, I still have a chance here.

Kyra A chance?

Tom Yes.

Kyra What sort of chance?

Tom I think you know what I mean. I kept on saying, if I behave well, if I get through this, then maybe Kyra is going to come back.

Kyra stands stunned, understanding how deep his feeling is. He goes on haltingly.

Sitting by the bed. Just awful. Looking at Alice, propped up on the pillows, her eyes liquid, cut off . . . I'd think, oh shit, if Kyra were with us, if Kyra were here . . . (*He stops a moment and shakes his head.*) Jesus, why weren't you? 'If Kyra were here, she'd know what to do.'

Kyra stands absolutely taken aback as if not knowing what to think about his shocking devotion to her. He knows how much this has affected her.

You told me, you said, always be honest. Look life in the eye. Be courageous. Don't be afraid. But you ran and left us.

Kyra Yes. I had to.

Tom You did what you said people never should do.

Kyra I had no alternative. I had to get out of Alice's way. I had to make a new life of my own.

Tom And this is it, Kyra? This is the life that you made? Will you tell me, will you tell me, please, Kyra, what exactly are you doing here?

Suddenly there are two shocked people in the room. She is holding the edge of the table. When she speaks she is very quiet.

Kyra Are you going to go down? Will you speak to Frank then?

Tom What shall I say to him?

Kyra Send him away.

Without looking at her Tom walks across the room and opens the door and goes out. Kyra is alone, dazed now, white, like a shadow. She goes into the kitchen and pours the sauce into a bowl. She puts the bowl on the table, mechanically, not really thinking. She puts a second wine glass on the table. Then she gets a loaf of bread, takes a

53

knife and cuts slices. The room seems dark, like a painting, the little red fire burning and the shadows falling across her face. Then Tom appears at the door. He closes it but does not yet move towards her.

Tom He's gone.

He moves across the room. They take each other in their arms and she holds him tightly, hugging him desperately, and beginning to cry, shaking with grief in his arms. He puts his hand through her hair.

Kyra, Kyra I'm back.

He runs his hand over and over through her hair. The lights fade to darkness.

Act Two

SCENE ONE

The door to the bedroom is slightly ajar. A white light, reflected off snow, comes from outside the kitchen window. The bar heater Kyra lit hours ago is still on, and glowing. It's around 2.30 a.m.

Kyra appears in the doorway. She is wearing a white flannel nightdress, over which she has put a sweater and a cardigan. She has clearly just woken up. She moves across the room trying to make as little noise as possible. The tray of cutlery she threw earlier is still scattered all over the floor. The abandoned meal is still on the table, uneaten. She looks at it a moment, then takes the spaghetti sauce she made earlier, picks up a piece of bread, then carries them both across the room. Kyra puts them down by the big armchair, then looks for the school exercise books which she had put on the floor for the meal. She picks them up, then turns on a low side-light. She pulls the little heater nearer the chair, then sits down with it at her feet. She puts the books on her knee, then dips her bread in the cold sauce and starts to eat.

This is how Tom finds her as he now appears in the doorway of the bedroom. He has put on his shirt and trousers, but his feet are bare. He stands a moment, trying to make sense of the scene in front of him: the teacher sitting with books on her knee, the glow of the heater on her face.

Tom What are you doing?

Kyra Eating the sauce. I'm starving. Remember? We never had supper.

Tom God, I'm sorry. I fell asleep. What time is it?

Kyra I think it's two-thirty.

Tom I must say . . .

Kyra It's no worry. I must have fallen asleep as well.

She looks at him, genuinely affectionate. He moves towards her, an easy warmth between them, and kisses the top of her head in the chair.

Tom Why don't Baptists like to fuck standing up? Because they're frightened God will think they're dancing. Is it me? Or has something happened to make it warmer in here?

Kyra looks up, amused. He wanders away, more skittish, definitely pleased with events.

Kyra It may be you. But also it's snowing finally. Everything's covered in snow.

Tom My God, you're right. It's beautiful. I'm beginning to like it. I think I've decided I'm going to move in.

Kyra just sits back, as he looks round, comfortably at home.

I was lying there, yeah, in that bed of yours, next to that sort of interesting lump in the mattress you have, I was thinking I could get used to this. Maybe this area isn't so bad. Over there, I was thinking, I'm going to put my telly . . .

Kyra Have you still got that big one?

Tom Oh no. It's much bigger now. I've got a home projection system. Enormous. It's going to take up most of that wall. (*He points to her wall of books, then looks round contentedly, imagining the scene.*) Yes. The football. Sunday afternoons with the lager . . .

Kyra Do you still support Chelsea?

Tom Of course.

Kyra How are they?

Tom They play the English game. My own game, you know. Kick it up the middle and hope for the best. (*He is amused, knowing how perfectly the sentiment suits him personally.*) And over there, the stereo. Maybe put Frank in a box-room. He'd love it. We could make a life, you and me. Take-away Indians . . .

Kyra Except you'd need the house next door as well to store all your clothes.

Tom Oh no, I've stopped all that rubbish. I haven't bought clothes . . . well, since Alice died. Do you think I've lost weight? A diet of suffering . . . (*He does a little pirouette.*)

Kyra I didn't notice, in fact.

Tom No.

Kyra I wasn't thinking.

Tom I was thinking, whatever else happens, we always have this.

> *Tom has said this speculatively, but Kyra says nothing. She is curled up in the chair, at peace. She puts her bread back in the sauce and starts eating again.*

I was wondering, you know, it can't be much longer. Your term.

Kyra No. There's only two weeks to go.

Tom Do you know what you're doing for Christmas? It's just I've now got this place in the sun. It's at the water's edge. It's perfect. The steps lead down to the sea. The island has palm trees. Beaches. Great fish. Unless of course you'd made other plans . . .

57

But Kyra still doesn't answer, just dipping her bread in the sauce.

I mean I'm just saying. Think about it.

Kyra Yes.

Tom No pressure.

Kyra No.

Tom No hurry.

Kyra Of course.

Tom If you let me know, say, Friday. No, honestly, that's just a joke.

They both smile, liking his half-serious, half-funny tone.

For God's sake, I'm not totally insensitive, I don't think 'one fuck and everything's solved . . .'

Kyra has got up to go to the kitchen to put the kettle on and now passes him.

Kyra Two, though, and that'll be different.

Tom (*smiling*) I mean, well, yes. That sort of thing.

He's pleased with the way this is going. He is at ease in the flat, casually looking at papers on her desk.

Kyra Why so long? I mean, till you came round here?

Tom No well, I suppose . . . I suppose the feeling of needing you . . . not easy to admit when you get to my age. Also I've been very busy.

Kyra Oh, well then . . .

Tom I'm only half-joking. I do have to work twice as hard. The company's been radically restructured . . .

Kyra Ah, yes, then obviously . . .

Tom There's been a refinancing package as well . . .

Kyra Do you ever think of leaving? Just packing up and living in your place in the sun?

Tom I've thought of it. Of course, if I'm honest. But the problem is, I'm not sure I want to go by myself. I've always had someone there. I actually need a woman to worship.

Kyra Oh come on . . .

Tom Oh, of course, I know you're not meant to say that . . .

Kyra Tom, it isn't just saying it, it's also using that word.

Tom protests, but Kyra is already moving back into the room, as if even he could not be so ignorant.

Tom What word?

Kyra Even you must have realized. When a man says he worships you, he's building a scaffold. It's a matter of time till he claims that you've let him down.

Tom looks puzzled at how she has reacted to what he felt was just a chance remark.

You should get out more! Recently, I tell you, there's been a whole group of us . . .

Tom Really? What sort of group is this?

Kyra It's more a sort of . . . informal gaggle of friends. We meet after work on a Friday. We meet and we all have a drink. There's a couple of teachers. And Adele. She's from Zimbabwe. And we talk, you know. Like one girl is a hairdresser. Another one works in a shop.

Tom And you meet every Friday, so you can have a good laugh about men?

Kyra refuses to take his hostility seriously.

Kyra Oh, come on, no, look, it's just casual.

Tom Thank goodness.

Kyra It's nothing, for God's sake, it's just hanging out. I've developed this passion for listening.

Tom Blimey.

Kyra Yes. It's like an addiction. I love it. I can't get enough. And the more I listen, the more it strikes me, you know . . . well, what extraordinary courage, what perseverance most people need just to get on with their lives.

Tom Huh.

Tom watches as she moves round the room, laughing at herself, becoming more expansive.

Kyra I know it sounds crazy, but I'm out at six-thirty – earlier . . .

Tom My goodness!

Kyra I get on the bus. That simple journey, I promise you, Kensal Rise to East Ham, in many ways it's the best thing in my life. I take a good book. I take my sandwiches. Every day I sit there. Always the top. The top deck's better.

Tom Oh, really?

Kyra Always. You hear better things.

Tom When I travelled by bus, I just used to hear people moaning.

Kyra Well, yes, there is some of that. But people . . . you know, the point is, they're so much smarter . . . this is the point. This idea they're all sitting there, everyone watching TV every night, in some sort of vegetable state . . .

Tom Aren't they?

Kyra Not at all, no.

Tom You could have fooled me.

Kyra People discriminate. It's quite extraordinary. You listen, and they have bullshit detectors working full time.

Tom is looking at her, amused by her faith in humanity, but she has already gone on, a new sunniness in her.

There was this guy the other day, I was riding next to him, actually it turned out I'd seen him at the school . . .

Tom What does he do?

Kyra Oh. He's in security. He works in this private security firm.

Tom At the school?

Kyra Yes. I mean, we've had them there lately. Just for a few days. It was absolutely disgusting, the staff protested like mad . . .

Tom is looking at her. But she doesn't get flustered, she just goes on explaining.

We had this problem with burglary. Lootings. A dinner lady was mugged.

Tom She was mugged in the school?

Kyra Tom, that's not unheard off. Don't take up that Home Counties tone.

Tom I'm not. Just allow a moment of tax payer's interest that dinner ladies now walk in fear of their lives.

He is making a joke, but she quickly corrects him.

Kyra One dinner lady.

61

Tom OK.

Kyra Only one incident. It happens. It happened once. But of course it's being used politically. There are – let's face it – certain elements. Partisan elements, who wish the school ill.

Tom For what reason?

Kyra Precisely because it is an enlightened regime. It's just a piece of street theatre. Putting these baboons in blue uniforms, out there in front, by the gates. They're there to destroy parents' confidence, to make them feel discipline's somehow collapsed.

Tom Oh I see. And has it?

Kyra No. No, of course not.

Tom You were telling me earlier . . .

Kyra I mentioned certain events. These events occurred in a context. You'd have to be there, you'd have to take part in the life of the school to know exactly how much significance to attach to these things.

Tom just looks at her, saying nothing. But she protests more strongly.

Tom, don't look at me like that. I'm not a soft liberal.

Tom I didn't say anything.

Kyra Far from it. My views have got tougher. They've had to. You grow up pretty fast. Education has to be a mixture of haven and challenge. Reassurance, of course. Stability. But also incentive.

Tom I'm not sure I actually know what that means.

But Kyra ignores his humour, really forceful and coherent, wanting to explain.

Kyra Tom, these are kids from very tough backgrounds. At the very least you offer them support. You care for them. You offer them security. You give them an environment where they feel they can grow. But also you make bloody sure you challenge them. You make sure they realize learning is hard. Because if you don't . . . if you only make the safe haven . . . if it's all clap-happy and 'everything the kids do is great' . . . then what are you creating? Emotional toffees, who've actually learnt nothing, but who then have to go back and face the real world.

She is genuinely carried away with this problem as she gets another piece of bread to dip in the sauce. Tom is watching her as non-judgementally as he can.

I mean . . .

Tom I see that.

Kyra I tell you, it's fucking interesting . . .

Tom I'm sure . . .

Kyra Finding that balance . . .

Tom Sure . . .

Kyra Finding it, keeping it there. Tom, there's nothing I've done in my life which is harder. Forty per cent speaking English as a second language! It stretches you, it stretches you as far as you'll go.

She stands cheerfully dipping bread in the sauce.

Tom (*a little shocked*) You're really that involved?

Kyra You mean me personally?

Tom Do you go to staff meetings?

Kyra I'm not an activist, if that's what you mean. But I

63

take it quite seriously. Because . . . apart from anything
. . . I'm older than most of the teachers . . .

Tom Really?

Kyra It's a young person's area. A young teacher comes out
of college. They think, this is the kind of work I want to do.
Then pretty soon . . . well, they move house, they marry . . .
They decide they want something a little bit easier.

Tom Mmm.

Kyra A little bit less arduous. Mostly.

Tom But that's not happened to you?

*Kyra thinks a moment, then speaks thoughtfully, her
tone hardening.*

Kyra Early on, you know, I was spat on. Very early. Like
maybe, the first day or two. In front of the class, this boy
spat on me. He called me an arsewipe. A cunt. I tell you, I
can still feel it. Here, on the side of my cheek. I realized I
had no defences. That night I went home and I cried. Then
I thought, right, this is it. No more crying. From today I
learn certain skills – survival skills if you like. I master
certain techniques, if for no other purpose but that in the
years ahead . . . maybe even after I've finished perhaps . . .
I can say, right, it was a job and I bloody well did it. I
learned how you have to survive.

Tom I see. It sounds like a challenge.

*Kyra hesitates, deciding whether to risk saying what she
actually believes.*

Kyra I've seen the way things now are in this country. I
think for thirty years I lived in a dream. I don't mean that
unkindly. Everything you gave me I treasured. But the fact
is, you go out, you open your eyes now, you see this
country as it really is . . .

She shakes her head slightly, then waves her hand, as if to imply that nothing more can be said. Tom is watching, suddenly chilled, fearing he has lost her.

Tom But you have friends?

Kyra What?

Tom This life that you're leading? I'm asking, it's not without friends? It's none of my business, but as you describe it . . . I suppose it all sounds a bit *bleak*.

Kyra Tom, the point is, we're mostly totally exhausted . . .

Tom I'm sure.

Kyra What are you asking? Do I go out? Oh yes, I go out! On Fridays, I go to Thank God It's Fridays. On Saturdays, Sainsbury's. And also, yes, I have a few friends.

Tom Well, good.

Kyra Adele is terrific. She lives downstairs. She's the woman who found me this place.

Tom You call that an act of friendship?

Kyra Oh very funny.

Tom It's more like she's trying to freeze you to death . . .

But Kyra's up to this, off to the kettle, and already off on a tack of her own.

Kyra It doesn't bother me. Not after my childhood.

Tom Being pushed by nannies beside stormy English seas . . .

Kyra My dreadful father had something he called heating bill targets. He'd hold up the heating bills, he'd say, 'By all means, keep this place like a furnace, if that's what you

65

want. But remember: turn it up in September, by February you'll have to be turning it down . . .'

Tom smiles at this.

You know he died?

Tom When?

Kyra Yes. A year ago. Dropped dead on the golf course.

Tom But, Kyra, I don't understand. I thought you were going to get lots of money.

Kyra Ah, well, yes, I thought so as well.

Tom *So?*

Kyra Tom, things are never that simple. This is also a man who kept cats.

Tom Oh come on . . .

He turns away in disbelief, but Kyra is laughing, somehow exhilarated by the account of her father's behaviour.

Kyra It's true. He gave me some money. Not much. In fact, very little. The RSPCA got nearly all of it.

Tom But for Christ's sake, how did you *feel*?

Kyra I didn't feel anything. What difference did it make?

Tom I'd have thought all the difference.

Kyra What do you mean?

Tom frowns, as if it were obvious, not sure why she doesn't get it.

Tom If you'd had his money you would have been able to buy a new place.

Kyra Oh.

Tom I mean, *that's* what I'm saying. You would have been able to leave. You could have bought somewhere decent.

Kyra I mean, yes, I suppose so . . .

Tom You can hardly intend to live here the whole of your life? I suppose I'm asking, what are you planning?

Kyra Planning? Tom, I don't expect this to make any sense to you. But I'm planning to go on just as I am.

She has said what she wanted quite simply, but somehow in the very quiet of the moment there is a sense of challenge. She moves back to the kitchen, in order not to have to deal with his response. Neither of them mistake the fact that a crucial moment has been reached.

Do you want tea?

Tom What?

Kyra Shall I make tea for you?

Tom Tea? Oh, yes. I mean, yes. Of course.

Kyra is putting tea-bags in the pot. He is trying to keep his tone normal.

I don't know. I know it sounds silly. There's something . . . I suppose, an idea of the future. It seems to me important.

Kyra Why, sure. I have an idea of the future as well.

Tom Do you?

Kyra Yes. Yes, I mean loosely. A future doing a job I believe in. (*She sees he is still unhappy, his pain undischarged.*) Why does that bother you?

Tom Because of a feeling . . . it's to do with something that happened with Alice. Something which happened right at the end.

*Kyra stands, milk carton in hand, seeing his pain,
knowing she must let him speak.*

Do you know how I first met her? I saw her modelling in a
magazine. I thought, oh look, it's Audrey Hepburn.

Kyra You cut out her picture. That's what I heard.

Tom I sent her flowers. Red roses. I sent her these roses,
day after day. After a month of this, she finally agreed to
meet me. In a coffee shop. She was quite charming. Quiet,
you know. But she said, 'I'm not a thing, don't you see?
You can't buy me. Whatever you give me, I can't ever be
bought.' I remember, even then, I was just laughing. I said,
'My God, do you not understand?' (*He has become
expansive, his old energy back as he tells this story, as
well as a genuine indignation about his motives.*) You see,
by that time, I'd already started. I had a couple of
restaurants, nothing too grand. But I'd already worked out
– I'm not an idiot – you either run money or else it runs
you. If you keep your money . . . if you're frightened to
spend it, you become its prisoner. OK, sure, when you're
making it, be as mean as you like. But when you spend it,
just give. Give. Show your contempt for it. I said to her,
there in that café, 'I give for the pleasure of giving. Just for
the pleasure itself.'

Kyra But Alice understood that.

Tom No. She never accepted it. I promise you. Right to
the end. She always thought if I was giving, then somehow
I must want something back.

*Kyra is beginning to understand now, instinctively
knowing where he's heading.*

Kyra You told me you built her that room to be ill in.

Tom That's what I'm saying. Exactly. That's what I mean.
I gave it to her because . . . oh shit . . . I preferred it that

she should be happy. What's wrong with that? I wanted
her to die in a place that she liked.

He goes across the room and takes the whisky bottle.
He pours himself a scotch, which he does not yet drink.

While she was dying, every night I brought her these
flowers. The very same flowers – red roses – that I'd given
when we first met. Then one day she was lying, her head
on the pillow, I thought asleep. She suddenly said, 'No. No
more flowers.' I said, 'Why not?' She said, 'It isn't the
same.' She said, 'The flowers were when you loved me.
You and I were really in love.' She said, 'Now I don't want
them.' (*For a moment there are tears in his eyes, his grief*
almost overwhelming him.) She was one week from dying.
Kyra, that's fucking hard.

Kyra Yes.

Tom I'd tried to explain to her . . . many times I'd tried to
talk about you. But she'd cut me off. She'd made up her
mind. She had her opinion. And believe me, she wasn't
willing to change. She knew exactly what she was doing.
The one thing she had was her moral authority. A wrong
had been done. That was it. The last thing she wanted was
to change her view of things, and certainly not by listening
to mine. (*He turns and looks at Kyra.*) She used her death
as a way of punishing me. (*Before Kyra can protest he*
holds up a hand.) No, really. Really! You think I'm
exaggerating. She treated me as if I were still some sort of
schoolboy: you betrayed me; that's it. Now in my opinion
that's not bloody fair. (*He moves away, bitter, his drink*
now in his hand, not looking at Kyra.) What I'm saying: it
wasn't one-sided. It wasn't simply that I was a shit. You
have to deal with this – part of the problem was Alice.
Right to the end, she couldn't forgive. And even now I feel
out on a limb.

Kyra I see that.

Tom I get home from the restaurants – that's if I bother to go in at all – at ten-thirty I think that I'm tired, but then two hours later I'm sitting up, stock still in bed. I go for a walk on the Common. Sometimes. I go out around three. Just looking around, and thinking. Always the same thought. I find myself thinking: something must come of all this. (*He knocks back his scotch in one, a wildness now starting to appear in him.*) I try to go out. I try to enjoy myself. I think: oh tonight, I'll go out, I'll get drunk. But my foot's on the floor, I'm pumping, I'm flooring that fucking pedal, and nothing's moving. I'm getting no fucking pleasure at all.

> *Sensing where he is heading, she is nervous. But he is gaining in strength, as if the worst of this confession is over.*

It's like, you know, like earlier you were saying, how all the time you felt you'd been loyal to her. You'd also been loyal to something inside yourself. I suppose I feel: what happens now? Do we just leave it? Just leave it completely? And if we did, isn't that like admitting our guilt?

Kyra Tom . . .

Tom No, look, isn't that like saying we did behave shabbily? And, oh it was just an affair! And then when she found out, it was over? Doesn't that seem to you wrong?

> *Kyra looks at him, then frowns, moving away a little. She is decisive, trying to be as serious as he was.*

Kyra Tom, you know there's something which you do have to deal with. There is this whole world I'm now in. It's a world with quite different values. The people, the *thinking* is different . . . it's not at all like the world which you know.

70

Tom looks at her, saying nothing.

I mean, if we ever . . . if we . . . what I'm saying . . . if we can work out a way of keeping in touch . . . then you have to know that I have made certain decisions. And these are decisions you have to respect.

Tom Why, I mean, yes.

Kyra Good.

Tom Surely. I'm not a complete idiot.

Kyra No.

Tom You're saying you've made an informed and serious choice.

A note of mischief is beginning to be detectable. Kyra looks at him suspiciously.

You've chosen to live in near-Arctic conditions somewhere off the North Circular. No, really. Why should I have any problem with that? (*He is beginning to get into his swing, exaggeratedly gesturing round the room now as he pours himself more scotch.*) I promise. I'm deeply impressed with it. I assure you, it gives me no problem at all. Put a bucket in the corner to shit in, and you can take hostages and tell them this is Beirut!

There is suddenly some savagery in his voice, but Kyra has decided to stay calm and not be bullied.

Kyra Tom, I have to tell you, this place is really quite reasonable.

Tom Oh really?

Kyra As it happens, I get it at a very cheap rent.

Tom I should hope!

Kyra It's you, Tom. The fact is, you've lost all sense of reality. This place isn't special. It's not specially horrible. For God's sake this is how everyone lives!

Tom Oh please, please let's be serious . . .

Kyra I mean it.

Tom Kyra, honestly . . .

Kyra No, this is interesting, this is the heart of it. It wasn't until I left your restaurants . . . those carpaccio and ricotta-stuffed restaurants of yours . . . it wasn't till I deserted that Chelsea milieu . . .

Tom Which in my memory you liked pretty well . . .

She stops, not at all put off by his interruption.

Kyra I do like it, yes, that isn't something I'd ever deny . . . but it wasn't until I got out of your limousines . . . until I left that warm bubble of good taste and money in which you exist . . .

Tom Thank you.

Kyra It was only then I remembered most people live in a way which is altogether different.

Tom Well, of course.

Kyra And you have no right to look down on that life!

Tom You're right.

Kyra Thank you.

Tom Of course. That's right.

Kyra waits, knowing this will not be all.

However. In one thing you're different. I do have to say to you, Kyra, in one thing you're different from everyone else in this part of town. You're the only person who has fought so hard to get into it, when everyone else is desperate to get out!

72

Kyra All right, very funny. For as long as I've known you, you've loved this.

Tom Loved what?

Kyra Whenever I say anything serious, there's nothing you like more than winding me up.

Tom Yes, I'm afraid that is true. But it's hard to resist winding people up when they've little metal keys sticking out of their backs.

Kyra And what does that mean?

But Tom is already moving across the room to pour himself a whisky, feeling himself on top in the argument.

Tom OK, you're right. I know nothing about anything. As you would say, I'm pampered. I admit it. Frank drives me round. But even I know that East Ham is on one side of London, and this place we're now in is somewhere quite else!

Kyra So? That is just chance.

Tom Oh really?

Kyra That's just how it happened. A friend found this flat! Adele was desperate. She was in the most desperate straits.

Tom just gives her a blank, sardonic stare.

All right, I admit it wasn't exactly convenient . . .

Tom It was sort of a sacrifice, is that the word? You work in one dreadful place. But of course for you, that's not nearly enough. You must punish yourself further by living in another dreadful place. And spend the whole day commuting between them!

Kyra Oh, for God's sake, that's not what I do.

73

Tom And, what's more, listening to the people on the journey, mopping up their every remark. As if they were Socrates, as if they were Einstein, just because they happen to travel by bus.

Kyra goes out to the kitchen to get the tea. But it doesn't stop him.

Remember? I come from bog-ordinary people, me. No solicitors hanging on my family tree! If you start out ordinary, I promise you, one thing you're spared, this sentimental illusion that ordinary people can teach you anything at all.

Kyra has been going to fill the teapot with hot water, but she is so provoked by him that she now comes out of the kitchen area, nodding vigorously.

Kyra I tell you, it's this, it's this that's so interesting. How you're threatened . . .

Tom Me, threatened?

Kyra Of course.

Tom By what?

Kyra I remember. As soon as any quite normal person is praised – a waiter, a chambermaid, someone who's doing a quite lowly job – you become like a dog on a leash. You can't wait for them to do something stupid, and great! you've found your moment to bite.

Tom That isn't true.

Kyra Oh, isn't it? (*But now it is her turn to feel confident*). I remember once saying I thought that Frank did his best to hide it, but underneath he was really quite bright. You said, 'Oh come on, let's face it, Kyra, there's a *reason* he's a driver . . .'

Tom Well what am I meant to say? You want me to lie? It's only the *truth*!

Kyra You don't talk to him. You don't ever talk to him.

Tom Frank? I talk to Frank. He tells me how Tottenham are doing, he tells me who Cindy Crawford is sleeping with now . . .

Kyra Oh, really!

Tom I mean, please. I'm not saying that Frank was born stupid. Believe me, I wouldn't say that. But if you turned him upside down, his brains would come out on the floor.

Kyra Why do you think I'm working where I am? I'm sick of this denial of everyone's potential. Whole groups of people just written off!

  But Tom is moving away, drinking, now thoroughly enjoying himself.

Tom Oh I see, right, you've been reborn. Now I understand you . . .

Kyra Tom . . .

Tom You see good in everyone now! How comforting! Of course. But if I could be reborn as anyone, I'm not sure Julie Andrews would be my first choice. (*Now it is Tom's turn to go through some sort of barrier, suddenly losing patience, at last wanting to put an end to things.*) I mean, Kyra, please! As you'd say: let's be serious! You must know what's happening. Jesus Christ, just look at this place! I mean, it is screaming its message. For instance, I tell you, look at that heater! Sitting there fulfilling some crucial psychological role in your life. There are shops, I mean, you know, *shops*, proper shops that exist in the street. These shops sell heaters. They are not expensive.

75

But of course they are not what you're looking for.
Because these heaters actually heat!

*Tom shakes his head, moving across the room to get
more scotch, reaching the real centre of his complaint.*

You accuse *me* of being a monster. You say that I'm guilty.
You tell me that I'm fucking up the life of my horrible son.
But the difference is at least I *admit* it. At least this evening
I took that on board. But you! Jesus! It's like talking to a
moonie. I've not set off like some fucking missionary to
conduct some experiment in finding out just how tough I
can make my own way of life.

Kyra You think that's what I'm doing? You really think
that's what this is?

*But Tom is already behaving as if it were all too
ridiculous for words.*

Tom I mean, I've been listening, I've been listening to this
stuff you've been telling me – the bus! the school! even the
kind of place that you choose to live in – and, I'm
thinking, my God, my dear old friend Kyra's joined some
obscure religious order. The Kensal Rise chapter! She's
performing an act of contrition. (*He suddenly laughs, the
next thought striking him.*) You say to me, Lord goodness,
everything's psychological. I can't be happy because I've
not come to terms with things that I've done. But you –
you're like Page One. A textbook Freudian study! Your
whole fucking life is an act of denial! It's so bloody clear.
You know what it's called? Throwing Teddy in the corner!
You're running so fast you don't even know you're in
flight.

Kyra Running?

Tom Yes. Of course. Yes, it's obvious.

Kyra I suppose you couldn't tell me. I'm running from what?

76

Tom Do I need to say?

His look, half-modest, half-arrogant infuriates her as much as his answer, and she turns away exasperated.

Kyra Oh honestly, this really . . . I mean, that is contemptible! Why do men always think it's all about them?

Tom Because in this case it is!

But Kyra never even reaches the kitchen before turning on him again.

Kyra I'll say this for you. You always understood procedure. You've always known the order in which things should be done. You fuck me first. *Then* you criticize my life-style . . .

Tom Now Kyra . . .

Kyra Doing it the other way round, of course, would be a terrible tactical mistake.

Tom All right, fair enough.

Kyra I mean, if you'd started by calling me weak and perverse, if you'd told me straight off I was fleeing from you . . . But the great restaurateur knows the order. You don't serve the pudding before the fucking soup!

She has said this with such venom that she now turns and goes to get their tea.

Tom I refrained from commenting only because it's so bloody obvious. I didn't actually think it needed to be said. You have a first-class degree, for Christ's sake.

Kyra Oh, really!

Tom You came out top of your year.

Kyra puts his tea down and stands by the table drinking her own.

I can't see anything more tragic, more stupid than you sitting here and throwing your talents away.

Kyra Am I throwing them away? I don't think so.

Tom Kyra, you're teaching kids at the bottom of the heap!

Kyra Well exactly! I would say I was using my talents. It's just I'm using them in a way of which you don't approve.

She has put down her tea and now goes into the darkened bedroom, leaving the door open.

Tom (*carrying on as if she were still there*) God, you claim *I'm* dismissive of people, you think I don't give them a chance. But any of those people who work for me . . . when they saw what you were doing with the gifts that God gave you . . . they would be so bloody furious.

Kyra (*off*) Would they?

Tom Of course! They wouldn't understand you, any more than I do. They would simply say you were shallow and spoilt. You know you could be teaching at any university. They'd take you today! Anywhere you liked! But oh no! Of course not, for Kyra, nowhere is good enough. Except of course somewhere that's no good at all . . . (*He stands, satisfied by his own irony, now becoming a generalized bad temper*.) Of course it's only this country, only here in this country, it's thought to be a crime to get on. Anything rather than achieve!

Kyra What you call 'achieve'!

She has appeared again in the bedroom doorway. She has dressed and put her jeans back on. He looks at her.

Tom Sitting in North London, just spinning your wheels. Out of stubbornnes. Sheer goddamned female stubborness.

Kyra 'Female'? That's a very odd choice of word.

He knows that he has betrayed a source of his anger and she at once has an ascendancy in the argument with him. She picks the books up off the floor and begins regretfully.

You see I'm afraid I think this is typical. It's something that's happened . . . it's only happened of late. That people should need to ask why I'm helping these children. I'm helping them because they need to be helped.

Tom turns away unconvinced by the simplicity of the answer, but she is already moving back to the table with the books, her anger beginning to rise.

Everyone makes merry, discussing motive. Of course she does this. She works in the East End. She only does it because she's unhappy. She does it because of a lack in herself. She doesn't have a man. If she had a man, she wouldn't need to do it. Do you think she's a dyke? She must be fucked up, she must be an Amazon, she must be a weirdo to choose to work where she does . . . Well I say, what the hell does it matter why I'm doing it? Why anyone goes out and helps? The reason is hardly of primary importance. If I didn't do it, it wouldn't get done.

She is now suddenly so passionate, so forceful that Tom is silenced.

I'm tired of these sophistries. I'm tired of these right-wing fuckers. They wouldn't lift a finger themselves. They work contentedly in offices and banks. Yet now they sit pontificating in parliament, in papers, impugning our motives, questioning our judgements. And why? Because they themselves need to feel better by putting down everyone whose work is so much harder than theirs. (*She stands, nodding.*) You only have to say the words 'social worker . . . 'probation officer' . . . 'counsellor' . . . for everyone in this country to sneer. Do you know what social workers do? Every day? They try and clear out society's drains. They clear out the rubbish. They do what no one else is doing, what no one else is willing to do. And for that, oh Christ, do we thank them? No, we take our own rotten consciences, wipe them all over the social worker's face, and say 'if . . .' FUCK! 'if *I* did the job, then of course if I did it . . . oh no, excuse me, I wouldn't do it like that . . .' (*She turns, suddenly aggressive.*) Well I say: 'OK, then, fucking do it, journalist. Politician, talk to the addicts. Hold families together. Stop the kids from stealing in the streets. Deal with couples who beat each other up. You fucking try it, why not? Since you're so full of advice. Sure, come and join us. This work is one big casino. By all means. Anyone can play. But there's only one rule. You can't play for nothing. You have to buy some chips to sit at the table. And if you won't pay with your own time . . . with your own effort . . . then I'm sorry. Fuck off!'

She has said this with such shocking brutality and callousness that Tom is stilled for a moment.

Tom All right, very well, I do see what you're saying.

Kyra I should hope so.

Tom This work you're doing leaves you deeply fulfilled.

Kyra flashes him a look of contempt.

But, Kyra, are you also saying you're happy?

Kyra Oh come on now, Tom, that isn't fair!

Tom Why not?

Kyra That's a shitty kind of question. You know. It's a game! I'm not playing that game!

But Tom has already moved away to get more whisky, his poise back and amused.

Tom The funny thing is – do you see? – you talk about escaping your father. You were always telling us. The chilly, cold childhood you had! But here you are, building exactly the same kind of bunker that he did . . .

Kyra Nonsense!

Tom Living exactly the same kind of isolated life. You end up here in this room. With ice on the windowpane. The wind still blowing off the bloody English channel. And no one allowed to get near . . . (*He is suddenly quieter.*) The only time you haven't been lonely, the only time you actually lived a proper life among friends, was when you lived in our family. And you know bloody well that is true.

Kyra doesn't answer, just looking at him as he moves away, sure of himself.

But now of course . . . *now* you'll do anything rather than admit it . . .

Kyra I know it's what you would *like* to be true.

Tom It *is* true.

Kyra On no account must I be happy. On no account must I have succeeded in getting away.

This is so near the mark that Tom just looks guilty, as she smiles, amused now at being able to satirize him.

You walk in this room, and at once you're picking up folders . . .

Tom What folders?

Kyra Glancing at the bookshelves. Lifting my papers. Oh my God, does she have a boyfriend?

Tom Oh, really!

Kyra Is there any trace of a *man*?

81

Tom I never did any such thing.

Kyra Looking for any male objects. Any gifts. Any ties. Any socks.

Tom Oh come on now, that's ridiculous.

Kyra Is it? Your whole body language expresses it. Ownership! I think you've patrolled this room fifty times. Inspected its edges. You even smelt the fucking bed! Like an animal. The whole thing's about possession.

Tom Kyra, you know that's not true.

But she is having too much fun to stop.

Kyra I mean, apart from anything, there is the arrogance, the unbelievable arrogance of this middle-aged man to imagine that other people's behaviour – his ex's behaviour – is always in some direct reaction to *him*.

She laughs now, going to get herself more tea and knowing she is building a formidable case.

Tom Well it is!

Kyra You were saying, my God! You were telling me you don't think of us as objects . . .

Tom I don't.

Kyra We're not possessions, that's what you say! Yet you stand there complaining your wife omitted to forgive you.

Tom She did!

Kyra I have to ask you, Tom, why the hell should she? When all the time you were dreaming of somebody else.

Tom All right.

Kyra I mean, Jesus . . .

Tom All right!

For the first time he is badly rattled. She is shaking her head in disbelief now.

Kyra Earlier this evening you were telling me that all the time she was dying you were meanwhile thinking about me! That's right! Yet you're standing there seriously demanding my sympathy for the terrible hurt which you're claiming *she's* done to *you*!

She has blasted him with this last phrase and he can't answer. So now she wanders away, so sure of her point that she laughs.

I mean, even you, Tom . . . even you must see it. I know, being a successful businessman – sweet wife, me adoring you as well! – you're richly deserving of compassion, I know your life was really jolly hard . . .

Tom All right. Very well . . .

Kyra But even you must see the balance of sympathy in this case maybe . . . just *maybe* lies somewhere else.

Tom You only say that because you weren't around.

At once Kyra turns impatiently, going to the kitchen, riled by the old accusation.

Kyra Oh, that again!

Tom Yes. Because that's at the heart of it. That's at the heart of all this.

Kyra Is that what you think?

Tom You know what I'm saying is right. You simply walked out! You simply walked out on me! That is a fact. (*He points a finger at her as if she were a wayward employee.*) And what's more, you did not consult me. You made a decision which I never approved.

Kyra (*at once not able to take his indignation seriously*)

83

Approved? You mean, you signed no consent form . . .?

Tom (*at once catching her tone*) All right . . .

Kyra You took no executive decision? You mean you never 'discounted' me, was that your phrase? I was never filed next to Alice. Diminishing assets!

Tom Oh, very funny. Oh yes, very smart!

He is moving away, nodding as if this is all too familiar for words. But she is enjoying herself, into a riff now.

Kyra You did not downsize me, delayer me, you did not have a drains-up meeting to discuss the strategic impact of letting me go? You mean I just went and there was no management buy-out?

Tom Oh, is this your idea of satire? And I suppose it's meant to be at my expense? (*He turns, only half-joking, his sense of humour departing.*) I knew this job of yours would make you a smartarse. Teacher! Of course. It's a joke. All teachers look down on business! They all mock business!

Kyra Tom, I'm just asking, but are you developing just a bit of a chip?

Tom Not at all.

Bad-temperedly he moves to get himself more scotch, but nothing will stop her now.

Kyra I mean, like earlier . . . earlier this evening, you were going on about 'business'. 'No-one understands *business*,' that's what you said. Suddenly, I must say, I hear it everywhere. These so-called achievers telling us they have a grievance. The whole of society must get down on their knees and thank them, because they do something they no longer call 'making money'. Now we must call it something much nicer. Now we must call it 'the creation of wealth' . . .

84

Tom looks at her uneasily, but she is really enjoying herself.

Putting money in your pocket. No longer the happy matter of just piling up coins. Oh no. We all have to say it's an intrinsically worthy activity. And the rest of us, we're ungrateful . . . we're immoral . . . we must simply be *envious* . . . if we don't constantly say so out loud. You have to laugh. It's this modern phenomenon. Suddenly this new disease! Self-pity! Self-pity of the rich! No longer do they simply accumulate. Now they want people to line up and thank them as well. (*She moves towards him, more serious now.*) Well, I tell you, I spend my time among very different people. People who often have nothing at all. And I find in them one great virtue at least: unlike the rich, they have no illusions that they must once have done something right! Nor do they suffer from delicate feelings. They don't sit about whining. How misunderstood and undervalued they are. No, they're getting on with the day-to-day struggle of trying to survive on the street. And that street, I tell you . . . if you get out there . . . if you actually have to learn to survive, well, it's a thousand times harder than leading an export drive, being in government, or . . . yes, I have to say, it's even harder than running a bank. (*She nods at this gentle reference to what he said earlier. She is quieter now.*) And the sad thing, Tom, is that you once knew that. When I first met you, you knew that full well. It marked you. That was the charm of you. It made you different. And I'm not sure the moment at which you forgot.

Tom looks at her.

Tom Well thank you.

Kyra Not at all.

Tom I needed that lecture.

Kyra It wasn't a lecture.

Tom It was good of you. Henceforth I'll try not to complain. (*He looks down, quietly self-mocking.*) Of course I'm disqualified from having any feelings, because I've made some money.

Kyra I didn't say that.

Tom No, you said something near it. For you, people are no longer people, it seems. Now they're symbols. And I am a symbol of . . . what does it matter? Something you're plainly angry with.

Kyra Oh come on, you know it's not as simple as that.

Tom (*not worried by her irritation, goes on unfazed*) I can see that you're furious. I'm not sure I wholly know why.

Kyra Come with me. Just spend a day with me. Then I think it will be pretty clear.

Tom Oh I'm sure. There's plenty of injustice. God knows, it's always been there. The question is why you've gone out to look for it. (*He is suddenly quite precise,*) I think it goes back to that day.

Kyra What day?

Tom The day Alice discovered.

Both of them know a decisive moment has been reached between them. Tom is quite calm, almost smiling.

You see, it's a funny thing, you've always said yes to everyone. It's something I noticed right from the start. Everyone liked you for this very reason. The first time they meet you, they always say, 'Kyra, what a nice person!' Always. 'Kyra, no question, she's a good sort . . .' (*He stops, gentle, knowing where he's going.*) It's typical. Your friend needs a tenant. To you, oh, it's no problem. You'll do it. There's no inconvenience. You're happy to do it. That's who you are. Even for us, when you started. You were happy to babysit when Alice and I wanted to go out. It used to amaze me. I used to ask myself why there was only one person, one person in the world my friend Kyra ever said no to. And that is the man who asked her if she'd be his wife.

Kyra sits silent, just looking at him.

I remember, I remember that morning so clearly. I remember coming downstairs. Then you were at the office. I rang you. I said, 'I'm afraid she's discovered. This is our moment. It's finally possible. So now at last we make a clean break . . .' You put down the phone. For the rest of the day I couldn't find you. At the office they said you'd simply walked out.

Kyra I did.

Tom Why? My marriage was finished. You knew that. And Alice herself had no wish to go on.

Kyra doesn't move, just watching.

Tom You could have had a thousand reactions. You could have gone to try and talk to Alice. You could have come to me. But no. You did something cowardly. You picked up your bags and walked out.

Kyra looks at him darkly, not answering.

Oh, you always said you did it for Alice.

Kyra Partly.

Tom That's what you told me. When I finally found you, you said, 'I had to do it. I did it for Alice. And for the children as well.' But that wasn't so. Well was it?

87

Kyra What do you want me to say?

*She looks at him resentfully, as if cornered. Tom
wanders away to get more whisky, having the
concession he wanted.*

Tom You didn't give a fuck about Alice's feelings.
Alice's feelings were just an excuse. I mean, even tonight,
you were telling me, you told me: an adulterous love is
the best. Well, let me tell you it isn't. The best thing is
loving with your whole heart. Yes, and what's more, out
in the open. The two of you. That's when there's risk.
Not the risk of discovery. But the risk of two people
really setting off on their own. But that means all the
things you've avoided. Really giving yourself. (*He has no
need to press his argument any more. His tone is
sorrowful.*) Even now you're doing it. You're telling me
how much you love the people! How much you're in
love with the courage of the people on the bus! Yes, of
course you love them. Because in three minutes you can
get off.

*Kyra stays sitting, stubborn now, her mood darkening
from sadness into resentment.*

Tom Do you think I don't see it? Loving the people's an
easy project for you. Loving a person . . . now that's
something different. Something that will take you right to
the brink.

Kyra That isn't fair.

Tom Isn't it? I think it is. You love the people because you
don't have to go home with them. You love them because
you don't have to commit.

Kyra (*quiet, not moving, looking down*) You're very cruel.
I've made a life here.

Tom Yes. You can't open a paper, that's what you say.

You have banished papers, you tell me, you've banished TV. I mean, why? What's the reason? It's some kind of insanity. What, you feel the world is somehow *letting you down*? You go off to do what you call 'rebuilding'. 'Rebuild your life', that's what you say. Start again. But how can you? Kyra, look at you now! It won't even work. It can't work. Because it's built on a negative. It's built on escape.

He shakes his head, genuinely infuriated now by her apparent passivity, sitting unmoving in her chair.

What is it in you? This thing that you have. Why doesn't it yield? I don't understand it.

Kyra No. I honestly don't think you do.

Her tone is icy. At last something has hardened in her. Tom tries to backtrack.

Tom Look . . .

Kyra You never will, Tom. It's the difference between us. It's kind of a gulf. (*She is deadly in her calm. She seems to be suppressing her strongest feelings.*) You're right. I've become my anger. (*She looks down.*) And now I think you should go.

Tom Go?

Kyra Yes. You got what you wanted. You wanted me to say I never loved you enough. Well, plainly, in your view, I didn't. And so that's the end of it. Isn't it?

She moves to the other side of the table where she takes up the pile of books. She puts them down, puts on her glasses, and calmly takes the first one to work on.

And these are books which I have to mark.

Tom is so inflamed by her control that he suddenly

loses his temper. He impetuously picks up the top book and throws it haphazardly across the room.

Tom Oh come on, these fucking books, these fucking children. Who are you fooling? Marking books in the middle of the night! Do you think that I'm fooled? You know what we had. Why can't you admit it?

He has screamed at her and picked up books and thrown them across the room. Because she does not respond, he picks up a couple more books. Then pushes over the pile. It is a gesture of mess and futility.

Kyra I think you should change.

Tom looks at her a moment, then he turns and goes into the darkness of the bedroom. Kyra is plainly shaken by what has just happened. She goes to the kitchen and pours herself a glass of water, which she drinks. She moves across to the sideboard and takes a small card out of a drawer. She then moves back to the telephone and dials a number.

Kyra (*on the phone*) Yes, hello. I'm at 43 Cannon Road. There's a friend of mine going to Wimbledon. (*Kyra listens.*) I understand that. A doorbell. Hollis. (*She waits a second.*) Thank you. Yes, as soon as you can.

She puts the phone down. She stands a moment, then goes to sit down again at the table. She is still for a moment. Tom comes back into the room in his suit, but carrying his shoes. They ignore each other as he sits down in an armchair to put his shoes on.

Kyra I got you a cab.

Tom Oh, all right . . .

Kyra I didn't suppose you were going to call Frank.

She looks kindly at him, trying to sound natural. But

*they are both shattered. It's past three and nothing
either of them intended has happened.*

They say they're not sure, but they think they can get
through the snow.

Tom By the time I get home it's going to be time to go into
work.

*He is now dressed. He looks a complete mess, his
clothes flung on, crumpled and untidy. She looks at
him, some genuine warmth in her voice.*

Kyra You look ridiculous. I'm afraid you've forgotten
your tie.

*She goes out into the bedroom to look for it. He looks
round the room for a moment, knowing it is the last
time he will see it. She comes back in and hands him his
tie. He takes it and goes over to a small mirror which
hangs over the kitchen sink. She sits at the table.*

You see, I remember the sequence. You ask me if I
remember that day. I remember the days before it. Why I
wrote those letters at all.

Tom shifts. She looks directly at him.

Do you remember why I had written?

Tom Of course. You went off on holiday,

Kyra Yes. For once, on my own. Because you two couldn't
come – I think a new restaurant was opening . . .

Tom That's right.

Kyra And I was exhausted. So I insisted. And you said,
'Kyra, you promise, whatever you do, you must
write . . .'

Tom They were wonderful letters.

Kyra I'm glad you thought so. I can remember, the first day going down to the beach and thinking . . . I am going to make this man very happy. I am going to tell him what he really wants to hear. It was also the truth. Even now, I remember, I remember writing 'You will never know the happiness you've given me. I'll never love anyone as I love you . . .'

She is so direct and simple that it is as if she is saying them right now for the first time.

After a few days, people on the beach were all looking and laughing. This strange English girl, I was chalk white, under a parasol, ordering just an occasional beer. (*She seems lost in the memory, but now she once more looks him straight in the eye.*) You say I can't give, that I've never given. I gave in those letters. I gave my whole heart. 'Just to think of you fills me with warmth and with kindness. All I want is that it should go on . . .'

Tom Yes.

Kyra I was on the beach, but I was in London, with you, as you tore at the envelopes, opening the envelopes with your big hands. I could see you. The overwhelming power of thought.

Tom stirs as soon as she resumes.

Then of course I got back. I said to you, 'Tom, those letters I wrote . . .' You said to me 'Yes, don't worry, it's fine, there's a safe in our house. It's upstairs in the attic. There's no reason Alice would ever go near . . .'

Kyra No.

Kyra Then, later, that morning. My first question to you on the phone: how did she find them? 'Oh,' you said . . .

Tom Sure . . .

Kyra Just for the night, you'd left them tucked away in the kitchen.

Tom That's right. (*He moves in, wanting to defend himself.*) But I told you, the night before I'd got them out to read them. I admit, I'd had a few drinks. Alice was asleep. I thought, I'm going to wake her if I go up to the attic. (*He stops a second, trying to make his explanation as smooth as possible.*) So I thought, just for this evening, I'll hide them in the kitchen. Then later I'll put them back.

Kyra But?

Tom Oh for Christ's sake, you know what happened. I was going out to work and . . . look, I don't know . . . Frank had been waiting, he was bullying me, telling me I had to hurry up. For whatever reason . . . I went off to work, and yes, I forgot!

Kyra You left them in the kitchen.

Tom Look, I'm not saying it was highly intelligent. I mean, at the time, I said it was crazy. I told you: it was stupid. It was remiss.

Kyra No, it wasn't remiss, Tom. It was deliberate.

There is a sudden silence. You can see Tom thinking how he is going to respond, whether to protest, or to consent.

Please, please don't start lying! Whatever you do, don't start lying to me!

Tom stands, chastened by her reaction. Then her own anguish begins urgently to appear.

Of course. Do you think I'm proud of it? Do you think it was easy? Just to walk out of your lives? Every day, I've thought of the wreckage, of what must have happened to

Alice and you. But I couldn't stay. I couldn't. Breeze in to Alice and say, 'Please understand, in my mind I never betrayed you. Really, I promise you, you have our everlasting love and respect . . .'? (*She smiles bitterly at the absurdity of it.*) Do you think we could have been happy? You and me? Happy like murderers, perhaps. And all the time I'd be thinking: the one thing . . . the one thing I asked him never to do . . . he went off and did it deliberately . . .

Tom Kyra, that just isn't true!

He turns away, knowing he cannot argue any more. And his concession calms her.

Kyra We had six years of happiness. And it was you who had to spoil it. With you, when something is right, it's never enough. You don't value happiness. You don't even realize. Because you always want more. (*She is beginning to be upset by what she is saying. He knows it is true.*) It's part of the restlessness, it's part of your boyishness. You say you knew that I loved and valued your family. You knew how much you were loved. But that can't be true. Well, can it? Because if you'd realized why would you have thrown it away? (*She looks at him, completely sincere.*) I love you, for God's sake. I still love you. I loved you more than anyone on earth. But I'll never trust you, after what happened. It's what Alice said. You'll never grow up. There is no peace in you. I know this. For me there is no comfort. There's no sense of rest. The energy's wonderful. Oh God, I tell you the energy's what everyone needs. But with the energy comes the restlessness. And I can't live in that way.

Tom (*serious now, pleading, unflinching*) You wanted a family. You say what you loved was family. I'm happy to start a family again.

Kyra No. It's too late. And you know it.

Tom Do I? Yes, I suppose that I do.

The doorbell rings. She turns and looks to it. They are both standing, some way between them. Tom does not move.

Tom The point is, I lived a long time next to cancer. Apart from anything it fucks up your brain. You start thinking things are deliberate. That everything's some kind of judgement. And once you think that, you might as well die.

The bell rings again. She opens the window to call down to the street.

Kyra He's coming.

But he does not move. She picks up the bag he brought the whisky in, and puts the remains inside.

Your whisky.

But he does not take it.

Tom I came here today, wanting forgiveness. I thought you'd say, well OK. Things do just happen, that's how it is. The world's not a court. Most things are chance. That's what I'm saying. A girl of eighteen walks down the King's Road . . . And in that girl, there's infinite potential. I suppose I just wanted some of that back.

His appeal to her has been so sincere and from the heart that she cannot answer. The bell rings again. Tom smiles grimly, giving way to the inevitable.

I'm sorry. I should pick up those books of yours.

Kyra Leave them. Honestly, really, it's fine.

He moves across the room and kisses her on the cheek.

Tom Goodbye.

Kyra Goodbye, then.

Tom looks at her a moment, then moves to the door, but turns back before he goes.

Tom At least, if nothing more, come to one of the restaurants. There are one or two which are really not bad. I promise you, you know, on a good night, it's almost as nice as eating at home.

He turns without looking at her and walks out of the room, closing the door behind. She listens to the sound of him going off down the stairs. She looks a moment round the room, turns out the lights, then goes across to the little heater, and pulls the plug out. The red glow dies.

SCENE TWO

From the darkness, morning light begins to shine at the window. It is in a small white square, throwing eerie shadows across the chilly room. Nothing has moved from last night. There is a desolation of bottles and glasses, the remains of the spaghetti, the abandoned tray of cutlery on the floor and the schoolbooks still scattered over the carpet. The room looks wrecked. Already there is a loud banging, knocking and ringing at the downstairs door. After a moment or two, Kyra comes flying through from the bedroom, pulling on her clothes as she comes. She has managed to get her jeans on, and is now just piling on sweaters and shirts. She has plainly been woken up by the racket as she comes through at amazing speed.

Kyra All right, for Christ's sake, what is it? I'm coming. What the hell's going on? (*She goes out the room. We can hear her going downstairs and opening the door. Off*) Oh, I don't believe it.

Edward (*off*) Surprise!

Kyra (*off*) What are you doing here? What have you got there? Come on, don't stand out there freezing.

The sound of the door being closed and them scrambling together, laughing, excited up the stairs. Their cheerful early morning vitality contrasts with the sombre mood of the previous scene.

Edward (*off*) It's kind of a joke. I just hope I can get it upstairs.

Kyra (*off*) Well, I must say!

There is a moment, and then the two of them appear. Edward, wrapped in scarves, is carrying an enormous styrofoam box which he has trouble getting in through the door. It is a couple of feet wide and a foot high, and appears to be heavy. Edward is talking as he comes in. Kyra follows.

Edward I don't know, at the time it seemed funny . . .

Kyra Just put it down over here. (*She is laughing as she closes the door and clears the central table for him to put the box down.*) Jesus, what time is it?

Edward I was frightened I'd miss you. I was frightened you'd already be gone.

Kyra Christ almighty, I've overslept. (*She has found a little clock in the middle of the night's debris.*) It's almost seven o'clock . . .

Edward I don't know. Perhaps this is a crazy idea. (*He has put the box down in the middle of the table. Rather sheepishly he mimes a fanfare with a little tooting noise.*)

Kyra I don't know what it is.

Edward I've brought you breakfast. You said you missed breakfast more than anything else.

Kyra Oh, Edward, I don't believe it.

Edward So here it is! (*He opens his arms like Dandini, a young man half full of pride, half embarrassment.*) You make a wish and it's here.

> *Kyra stands watching as at once he moves towards the box to take its lid off. Inside the large box, there are various smaller ones, either for refrigeration or to keep things hot. But first, Edward takes out a linen tablecloth which he spreads over her table. There is a lighthearted gaiety in his manner, which seems to have changed from the previous night.*

I went to the Ritz. I've a friend. He's my best friend actually. He was at school with me. He works in the kitchen.

Kyra Is he in his gap year?

Edward He is.

> *They smile at last night's joke. Edward is now getting out a load of Ritz silver – knives and forks, pudding spoons, salt and pepper pots, and an ornate butter dish.*

And he smuggled me this stuff. All this silver. Apparently they lose thirty ash-trays a week. People put them in their pockets. Still, that's how the rich stay rich, I suppose. Look – a real butter dish with proper ice cubes.

Kyra Unbelievable.

Edward I'm afraid the toast's a bit hard.

> *Edward has got out a silver toast rack with the toast all ready ranged on it. He is working at great speed and with considerable accomplishment. Kyra is so taken aback that she does not move, just watches delighted as he works like a professional waiter, laying the china now.*

Charentais melon. The orange has been freshly squeezed.
Marmalade. And there are croissants. At least I know the
coffee is hot. (*This, because it is in a silver thermos, which
Edward now opens. Then he takes another silver dish
from the hot box and opens it.*) The eggs are scrambled.

Kyra Fantastic.

Edward Well, they looked pretty nice when they left.

Kyra It doesn't matter. We'll eat them. Oh this is wonderful!

Edward Bacon. I thought you'd be pleased.

Kyra I didn't eat last night.

*But Edward doesn't hear this because he has taken out
the last pieces of linen and is moving towards her with
them in his hand.*

Edward And look, the *pièce de résistance*. Just smell the
napkins.

Kyra Yes, they're incredible.

*Kyra is suddenly overwhelmed and throws her arms
round Edward, holding him close, the tears pouring
down her cheeks.*

Oh, Edward, thank you. Thank you so much.

*She holds on to him, not wanting to let him go. After a
few moments, he quietly detaches himself, and she
wipes her cheeks.*

Edward Hey, look, I mean, it's just breakfast. I've just
brought you breakfast.

Kyra I know.

*Now he puts a small vase with a rose in it between
them as the last touch. The table looks perfect. It all
seems to have happened in no time at all.*

99

Edward Are we going to eat it?

She smiles. The light is growing all the time at the window. As Edward moves to the table, Kyra sets about getting ready for work, gathering her things together, her mood transformed into a purposeful high humour.

Kyra I have to eat quickly. There's a boy I'm late for. I'm teaching him off my own bat. Extra lessons. Early, so early! I sometimes think I must be going insane. (*She laughs. She has thrown her things down on the chair and moved across to brush her hair in the little mirror in the kitchen area. She talks happily meanwhile as she does.*) I wake at five-fifteen, five-thirty. The alarm clock goes off. I think, what am I doing? What is this all about? But then I think, no, this boy has the spark. (*She throws him a nervous smile.*) It's when you see that spark in someone . . . This boy is fourteen, fifteen. His parents are split. He lives in this place I cannot describe to you. It's so appalling he has to go to the bloody common to work.

The light is still growing at the window as she shakes her hair, and then starts putting things in her bag for the day's work. Edward watches, diffident, standing by the table, slightly awed at her energy and sudden access of cheerfulness.

I mean, to be a teacher, the only thing you really have going for you . . . there's only one thing that makes the whole thing make sense, and that is finding one really good pupil. (*She has moved into the room, and seeing the abandoned schoolbooks on the floor, starts to pick them up and arrange them in a pile.*) You set yourself some personal target, a private target, only you know it – no one else – that's where you find satisfaction. And you hope to move on from there. (*She gathers the last books together on the floor. Then for no apparent reason she*

repeats what she just said.) And that is it, that's being a
teacher. One private target, and that is enough.

> *She is kneeling on the floor, suspended for a moment,
> completely still, completely isolated in her own
> thoughts, as if there were no one else in the room, no
> one else in her life at all. After a moment, Edward goes
> to behind one of the chairs he has set out at the table.
> Hearing him move, she quickly gets up.*

Edward Your chair.

> *Kyra puts the books down on a side-table and goes and
> stands where he wants her to sit in a little parody of
> waiters' manners.*

Kyra Are you ready?

Edward Yes. Yes, I'm ready.

Kyra Then sit.

> *Edward goes round to his side of the table, Kyra
> standing behind her chair waiting until he is ready as
> well, observing the formality.*

This looks terrific. Come on, Edward, let's eat.

> *They sit down opposite one another. He pours coffee.
> She reaches for some scrambled eggs and toast. They
> smile at each other occasionally, at ease, but saying
> nothing. Together, they start eating happily. The table
> looks incongruously perfect in its strange setting. As
> they eat contentedly, the light from the window fades to
> dark.*